EUL VERLAG

MANAGEMENT MEDIENGESTÜTZTER DIENSTLEISTUNGSINNOVATIONEN

Herausgegeben von Jun.-Prof. Dr. Thomas Kilian, Koblenz, Prof. Dr. Harald F. O. von Kortzfleisch, Koblenz, und Prof. Dr. Gianfranco Walsh, Jena

Band 1
Harald F. O. von Kortzfleisch, Rüdiger H. Jung und Markus Nüttgens (Hrsg.)
Web 2.0 für KMU-Netzwerke – Ein gestaltungsorientierter Ansatz zur Steigerung der Innovation und Selbstorganisation von Unternehmensverbünden
Lohmar – Köln 2011 ◆ 376 S. ◆ € 65,- (D) ◆ ISBN 978-3-8441-0060-0

Band 2
Gianfranco Walsh und Harald F. O. von Kortzfleisch (Hrsg.)
Management von Service Innovationen in Business-to-Business Märkten – Erfahrungen, Konzepte und Handlungsperspektiven
Lohmar – Köln 2012 ◆ 324 S. ◆ € 62,- (D) ◆ ISBN 978-3-8441-0111-9

Band 3
Christoph Sohn und Harald F. O. von Kortzfleisch
Citizensourcing mit dem Open Policy-Making Toolset – Konzept und prototypische Umsetzung
Lohmar – Köln 2012 ◆ 112 S. ◆ € 42,- (D) ◆ ISBN 978-3-8441-0159-1

Band 4
Stefan Kalms, Dorothée Zerwas und Harald F. O. von Kortzfleisch
Ubiquitous Entrepreneurship
Lohmar – Köln 2013 ◆ 132 S. ◆ € 43,- (D) ◆ ISBN 978-3-8441-0286-4

JOSEF EUL VERLAG

Reihe: Management mediengestützter Dienstleistungsinnovationen · Band 4

Herausgegeben von Jun.-Prof. Dr. Thomas Kilian, Koblenz, Prof. Dr. Harald F. O. von Kortzfleisch, Koblenz, und Prof. Dr. Gianfranco Walsh, Jena

Stefan Kalms
Dorothée Zerwas
Prof. Dr. Harald F. O. von Kortzfleisch

Ubiquitous Entrepreneurship

EUL VERLAG

Bibliografische Information der Deutschen Nationalbibliothek

Die Deutsche Nationalbibliothek verzeichnet diese Publikation
in der Deutschen Nationalbibliografie; detaillierte bibliografische
Daten sind im Internet über <http://dnb.d-nb.de> abrufbar.

ISBN 978-3-8441-0286-4
1. Auflage November 2013

© JOSEF EUL VERLAG GmbH, Lohmar – Köln, 2013
Alle Rechte vorbehalten

Umschlaglayout: Marius Rackwitz

JOSEF EUL VERLAG GmbH
Brandsberg 6
53797 Lohmar
Tel.: 0 22 05 / 90 10 6-6
Fax: 0 22 05 / 90 10 6-88
E-Mail: info@eul-verlag.de
http://www.eul-verlag.de

Bei der Herstellung unserer Bücher möchten wir die Umwelt schonen. Dieses
Buch ist daher auf säurefreiem, 100% chlorfrei gebleichtem, alterungsbestän-
digem Papier nach DIN 6738 gedruckt.

Table of Contents

List of Figures

List of Tables

List of Abbreviations

3DS	3 Day Startup
ARD	American Research and Development Corporation
A.D.	Anno Domini
cf.	To confer
CIP	Competitiveness and Innovation Framework Program
COSME	Program for the Competitiveness of Enterprises and SMEs
EFER	European Forum for Entrepreneurship Research
e.g.	Exempli gratia (*for example*)
EIL	Electronics and imaging laboratory
EIP	Entrepreneurship and Innovation Program
Engl.	English
ERP	Enterprise resource planning
etc.	Et cetera
EU	European Union
EXIST	Existenzgründungen aus der Wissenschaft
GEM	Global Entrepreneurship Monitor
Ger.	German
i.a.	Inter alia (*among others*)
IT	Information technology
MIT	Massachusetts Institute of Technology
OECD	Organization for Economic Cooperation and Development
p.	Page
PARC	Xerox Palo Alto Research Center
SME	Small and medium-sized enterprises
SMS	Short message service
St.	Saint

1 Impact, Meaning, and Challenges of Ubiquitous Entrepreneurship

The Global Entrepreneurship Monitor (GEM), a research consortium that collects and compares data regarding entrepreneurial activities, found that in 2012 only 5.3 percent of Germany's adult population actively tried to set up new businesses or were owners of young[1] firms (Sternberg et al. 2012, 6). According to the GEM, Germany is not an entrepreneurial country in international comparison (Sternberg et al. 2012, 9).

In comparison, in the United States, total early-stage entrepreneurial activity[2] is more than twice as high as in Germany (Sternberg et al. 2012, 9). One reason might be that the US followed the World Economic Forum's recommendation (2009, 24), which proclaimed in 2009 that ubiquitous entrepreneurship and innovation must permeate society. In the same year, Julius Genachowski (2009), former chairman of the US Federal Communications Commission,[3] first used the term "ubiquitous entrepreneurship" to label the intended omnipresence of entrepreneurship. The lack of efficient knowledge and technology transfer between universities and start-ups in Germany may be among the reasons why entrepreneurial activity has lagged there (Sternberg et al. 2012, 24). Therefore, the political implications of GEM's findings are to strengthen the knowledge and technology transfer between universities and industry, as well as increase practical education in universities (Sternberg et al. 2012, 25) and to promote entrepreneurship in Germany.

However, promoting entrepreneurship is not that easy since *"[...] it is a multifaceted phenomenon that cuts across many disciplinary boundaries"* (Low and MacMillan 1988, 140). Therefore, several articles discuss what entrepreneurship is and how it can be described (Hoselitz 1960; Hébert and Link 1989; Stevenson and Jarillo 1990; Bull et al.

---

[1] No more than 3.5 years old
[2] Total early-stage entrepreneurial activity rates working age individuals actively involved in business startups within the last 3.5 years (cf. Sternberg, et al., 2012, p. 9).
[3] *"The Federal Communications Commission regulates interstate and international communications by radio, television, wire, satellite, and cable in all 50 states, the District of Columbia, and US territories. It was established by the Communications Act of 1934 and operates as an independent US government agency overseen by Congress"* (Federal Communications Commission, 2013).

1995). Although *entrepreneurship* has not been defined, entrepreneurs are important for the economy because they are innovative (Iyigun and Owen 1998, 454; Wennekers and Thurik 1999, 34; Lee et al. 2004, 881) and contribute to economic growth (Wennekers and Thurik 1999, 34; Audretsch 2007, 64). Because most entrepreneurs are well educated (Wadhwa et al. 2009, 9) entrepreneurship should be promoted especially within academia so that entrepreneurship becomes omnipresent at universities and steers Germany toward becoming an entrepreneurial country.

1.1 The Problem of Ubiquitous Entrepreneurship

Even though ubiquitous entrepreneurship has been required for quite some time, only a few initiatives currently promote ubiquitous entrepreneurship in academia. Therefore, reasonable efforts are being made to promote the omnipresence of scientific entrepreneurship, but the idea behind ubiquitous entrepreneurship often is not sustainable. At this point, the first research problem arises: Ubiquity has never been investigated and its characteristics are undefined; therefore, the meaning of ubiquity in various research fields cannot be stated exactly.

Furthermore, because entrepreneurship is not yet entirely defined, transformation is also difficult. Simply transferring some characteristics of ubiquity from one field of research to entrepreneurship will fail because research in entrepreneurship is too broad with no uniform definition. Therefore, the second research problem emerges: Entrepreneurship must be categorized to create a theoretical classification as the basis for transferring the identified characteristics to scientific entrepreneurship.

Finally, one more problem arises: If ubiquity is undefined and entrepreneurship only partially defined, ubiquitous entrepreneurship also will be undefined. Until now, this term has been only a figure of speech.

1.2 The State of Research on Ubiquitous Entrepreneurship in Several Research Fields

This book focuses on three research fields: humanities, information technology (IT), and entrepreneurship. Therefore, the current state of research in the fields of humanities, IT, and entrepreneurship are described and research deficits are highlighted in this section.

1.2.1 Humanities

Within humanities research, ubiquity mainly occurs in three areas. First, in Christian theology, the ubiquity or omnipresence of God is discussed, and first evidences are found in the first century A.D. (Barnard 1964, 255). However, God's omnipresence was not addressed directly until the fifth century A.D. when God was first said to have omnipresent power (Schaff 2007, 140). During the following centuries, God was described with several attributes, which are often contradictory because they are based on the finite Aristotelian cosmos, among other reasons (Grant 1996, xviii).

Second, God's omnipresence plays a role in the other major religions, namely Islam and Hinduism. Ways in which Islam characterizes God's omnipresence can be found in the Quran. Although Islam cannot look back onto quite as long a history as Christianity, Allah is attributed as being omnipresent as well. Within Hinduism, first evidences of God's omnipresence can be traced back to the 11th century. Furthermore, God's omnipresence is a current topic of interest for Hindus (Thillainathan 2010, 73).

Third, ubiquity can be found in the area of law, where the phenomenon of legal ubiquity occurs as well as the principle of ubiquity. The first attributes godlike qualities to the king, while the latter is considered a figure of speech.

1.2.2 Information Technology

Nowadays, digital information is present almost everywhere because it can easily be stored and retrieved. In 2007, Martin Hilbert from the University of Southern California and Priscila López from Open University of Catalonia determined that humankind was able to store 2.9×10^{20} bytes and communicate almost 2×10^{21} bytes of information (Hilbert and López 2011). Clearly, IT plays a major role in modern society, and therefore it is necessary to research ubiquity in IT, where it occurs as ubiquitous computing, an area that carries ubiquity in its name.

To get a better understanding of ubiquitous computing, we must distinguish it from mobile and pervasive computing, terms that are often used interchangeably (Lyytinen and Yoo 2002, 63). Broadly speaking, high levels of embeddedness and mobility are characteristics of ubiquitous computing. In a detailed view, first efforts toward ubiquitous computing were made in the late 1980s in Palo Alto (Weiser et al. 1999, 693). Mark Weiser was a pioneer within this area of research because he described invisible computers working in the background for the first time (Weiser 1991, 94). In the early 21st century, Weiser developed his vision further, especially regarding context-awareness and trustworthiness.

1.2.3 Entrepreneurship

Entrepreneurship as a field of research provides insight into the qualities needed to be an entrepreneur. Although the history of entrepreneurship can be traced back to the Middle Ages, until now no uniform definition has existed. Using one specific definition always means leaving out other important parts of entrepreneurship because of its complexity. Nevertheless, Cuevas (1994) analyzed various definitions and derived three common spheres to characterize entrepreneurship. Besides the fact that entrepreneurship means different things to different people, it is extremely important to economics as well as society. As mentioned, most entrepreneurs are well educated (Wadhwa et al. 2009, 9), and therefore, can play a prominent role in academic discussions. However, within academia, a distinction must be made between academic and scientific entrepreneurship, with the entrepreneurial university playing a major role.

1.3 The Research Gap of Ubiquitous Entrepreneurship

In literature, the term *ubiquity* has never been analyzed interdisciplinary. In fact, the term can be found in several fields, for example in theology and in IT, although the range from one field to another has never been spanned. Thus, similarities between each field have not been identified. Finally, characteristics are missing, which make it possible to transfer the thoughts behind the term *ubiquity* from one field of research to another. If ubiquity is described in the fields of humanities and IT, then there might be impacts on entrepreneurship, too. However, these impacts are currently unknown and have not been researched. Finally, if these characteristics exist, a framework is missing to indicate how ubiquity can be reached in academia.

In summary, these three research questions are identified:

(1) **What are the characteristics of ubiquity in humanities?**

To answer this question, this book explores how ubiquity is attributed in theology and in the field of law. The characteristics are aggregated in tabular form for comparison.

(2) **What are the characteristics of ubiquity in IT?**

This research question explores the characteristics of ubiquity in IT, particularly ubiquitous computing. Again, these characteristics are aggregated in tabular for comparison.

(3) **How can characteristics from humanities and IT enable ubiquitous entrepreneurship?**

The results from the first two questions are evaluated to explore the answer to the last. The characteristics are used to create a framework consisting of both determinants and a ubiquitous entrepreneurship board, which increases the framework's practical application.

The next chapter outlines the book's structure, which arises from the deduced research questions.

1.4 Structure of the Book

The first chapter begins with an overview of the problem of ubiquitous entrepreneurship. Subsequently, the state of research on ubiquitous entrepreneurship in humanities, information technology, and entrepreneurship is discussed, the research gap in these fields is identified, and the structure of this book is formulated.

In Chapter 2, ubiquity in humanities is investigated. First, drawing on the etymology of the term ubiquity, the ubiquity of God in theology is analyzed, with a focus on the three major religions – Christianity, Islam, and Hinduism (see subchapter 2.1). Second, ubiquity in the field of law is investigated to examine whether and how ubiquity is described in jurisprudence (see subchapter 2.2). Third, subchapter 2.3 summarizes the identified characteristics, which can be used to describe ubiquity in the field of humanities. Moreover, the reasons why ubiquity in the field of law is less important than in theology are highlighted. Therefore, Chapter 2 answers the first research question.

Complementary to Chapter 2, which mainly focuses on history, Chapter 3 focuses on the field of IT, where ubiquity occurs in the area of ubiquitous computing. Hence, subchapter 3.1 describes the visionary idea of ubiquitous computing and its early development. Next, ubiquitous computing in the 21st century is described, and this knowledge is used to identify characteristics for ubiquity, based on the research in IT (see subchapter 3.2). Hence, Chapter 3 answers the second research question.

Chapter 4 establishes the basis for considering the third research question. In subchapter 4.1, all entrepreneurship theories are introduced to provide a brief understanding for why entrepreneurship is often described as a multifaceted phenomenon (Low and MacMillan 1988, 140) without a uniform definition. Subsequently, subchapter 4.2 identifies three main characteristics of entrepreneurship derived from entrepreneurial theories, which can be used to attribute entrepreneurship holistically instead of creating a limited definition. At the end of the chapter, the importance of entrepreneurship for the society and economic development today is emphasized (see subchapter 4.3). Furthermore, European entrepreneurial projects are briefly presented.

Chapter 5 deals with ubiquitous entrepreneurship in academia. Subchapter 5.1 describes how the university has developed during the first and second academic revolution and why it is important to promote the entrepreneurial university. Furthermore, the differences between academic and scientific entrepreneurships are described. Subchapter 5.2 highlights how the engineering paradigm is transferred to scientific entrepreneurship and presents the methods and instruments to be used within this holistic approach. Next, subchapter 5.3 describes how the characteristics of ubiquity, identified in chapter 2 and Chapter 3, impact the ubiquity of scientific entrepreneurship. Hence, the characteristics are used as determinants to develop a framework, consisting of a general framework and a ubiquitous entrepreneurship board, to reach ubiquity within academia. Based on those determinants, ubiquitous scientific entrepreneurship can be enabled using the developed framework. Accordingly, Chapter 5 answers the third research question.

Finally, chapter 6 summarizes the results of the book. Subchapter 6.1 draws conclusions concerning how to link the identified characteristics of ubiquity to ubiquitous scientific entrepreneurship. Furthermore, a description of this book's contribution to theory and practice is included. In conclusion, subchapter 6.2 presents further research that is needed based on the results in this book.

2 Ubiquity in the Research Field of Humanities

The etymology of the term *ubiquity* goes back to the late 16th century, and is derived from the neo-Latin word *ubiquitās*, which is a combination of the Latin word *ubīque* (everywhere) and the suffix *-itās* (English suffix: -ity) (Dictionary.com 2013). *Ubīque* itself is derived from the Latin term *ubī* and means *where* (Collins English Dictionary 2009). Thus, ubiquity can be interpreted as *"the state or capacity of being everywhere, especially at the same time"* (Dictionary.com 2013). The term's origin also can be found in Middle French, where the word *ubiquité* arose in the 17th century. In the time that followed, Harper (2010) stated that the meaning changed into *"turning up everywhere,"* first recorded in 1837, and originally meaning to be a jocular extension.

Ubiquity in Lutheran theology often refers to the omnipresence of God or Christ (cf. Richardson and Bowden 1983, 589; Fahlbusch et al. 1999, 258; Elwell 2001, 311), which leads to a wide field of research. Therefore, this chapter is divided into three parts. First, subchapter 2.1 takes a closer look at the divine's omnipresence in theology, exploring the three major religions' definitions of the divine's omnipresence. Second, subchapter 2.2 provides an outlook on how the concept of ubiquity is understood in the field of law, where it commonly is used in concepts such as *legal ubiquity* or the *principle of ubiquity* within jurisprudence. Finally, in subchapter 2.3, the characteristics are aggregated for the term ubiquity, and these are defined and evaluated in tabular form.

2.1 Ubiquity in Theology

Researching ubiquity in the field of theology requires analyzing the concept in several religions. As shown in Figure 1, the world's major religions are Christianity, Islam, and Hinduism. Fourteen percent of the world's population believes in other religions while 16 percent are nonreligious. Hence, about 84 percent of the world's population adhere to a religion. For reasons of simplification, this book concentrates on the three major religions to identify characteristics of ubiquity,[4] investigating whether and how these religions describe God's omnipresence. Accordingly, Christian theology is analyzed in subchapter 2.1.1, followed by Islamic and Hindu theologies in subchapter 2.1.2.

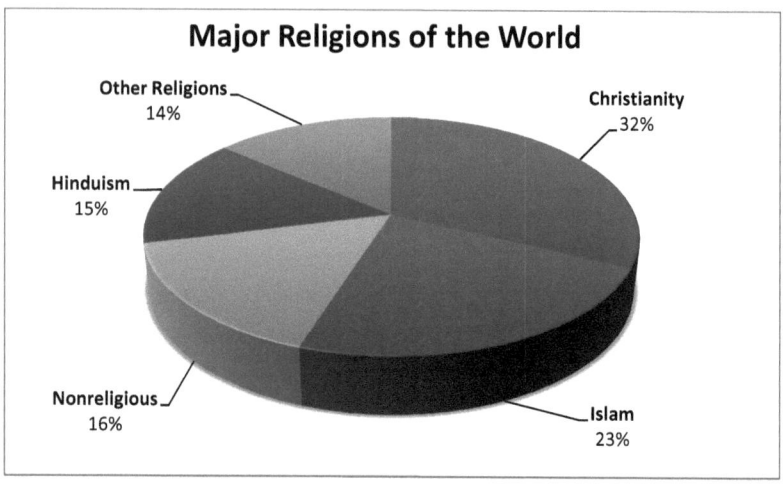

Figure 1: Major religions of the world ranked by percentage of global population (Source: Own representation based on Pew Research Center's Forum on Religion & Public Life [2012a])[5]

2.1.1 Christian Theology

First evidences of God's omnipresence can be traced back to the first century A.D. In the last decade of the first century, the Corinthian Church was *"[…] suffering from some grave internal dissensions"* (Barnard 1964, 255). Clement, bishop of Rome and author of the first epistle, reminds the Corinthian Church to avoid transgression. In Chapter 28 he states, *"[…] all things are seen and heard [by God] […]"* (Lightfoot 1889, 286).[6] This early Christian letter implies that if God sees and hears all things, then God,

---

[4] If 84 percent of the world's population belongs to a religion and the three major religions include 70 percent of all the faithful, the simplification made in this thesis considers more than 83 percent of all the faithful.

[5] The percentages slightly differ from the original source due to rounding.

[6] The First Clement, as the first epistle is also called, is also translated by Charles Hoole and Roberts-Donaldson. However, the 1868 translation by J. B. Lightfoot, professor at the University of Cambridge, is

or parts of God, must be present all around, although that statement is not written directly. Until the third century, scarce information can be found about God's omnipresence. Thus, Clement's first epistle has a great weight, which scholars duly recognize, according to Unnik (1951, 204).

In the third century A.D., further evidences appear. In *Against Praxeans,* early Christian writer Tertullian[7] mentions *"[...] that God is in the bottomless depths, and exists everywhere [...] [and] that the Son, being indivisible from Him, is everywhere with Him"* (Roberts and Donaldson 1870, 385). In contrast to Clement, Tertullian directly stated that God is everywhere. He also mentions that God is more than one, and combines the Father, the Son, and the Holy Spirit. However, God has not yet been directly described as *omnipresent.* This changed at the beginning of the fifth century when Augustine explained his idea of Christian society. He wrote 22 books to describe the God state in contrast to the earth state (Cranz 1950, 215).[8] In Book VII, Chapter 30, Augustine characterized the creator and the creatures, stating that God makes things as the same God and *"[...]is wholly everywhere, included in no space, bound by no chains, mutable in no part of His being, [is] filling heaven and earth with omnipresent power, not with a needy nature"* (Schaff 2007, 140). With this statement, God's omnipresence is described directly for the first time. Thus, in contrast to Tertullian, Augustine explained a more detailed and sophisticated view of God (Costa 2008, 86). An expanded discussion of the concept of God's omnipresence followed during the Middle Ages and into modern times (Costa 2008, 87).

Several other opinions describe different positions. For example, Saint Anselm[9] reflected on the attributes of God in his *Proslogium,* written between 1077 and 1078 (Topping 2002, 33). He concluded that omnipresence *"[...] is ultimately reducible to a kind of knowledge, immediate and localized for every region"* (Flint and Rea 2009, 201).

---

best known. All of them translate First Clement's Chapter 28 correspondingly: that God sees and hears all things (Kirby 2013).
[7] Quintus Septimius Florens Tertullianus, anglicized as Tertullian, is the first to describe God's trinity as the Father, the Son, and the Holy Spirit (Roberts and Donaldson 1870).
[8] The victory of King Alaric's Visigothic army over Rome in 410 impelled Augustine to write *De Civitate Dei,* or *The City of God* (Mommsen 1951, 346).
[9] Saint Anselm (1033–1109), Archbishop of Canterbury between 1093 and 1109, suggested ontological arguments in his *Proslogium* to prove God's existence (Christian Classics Ethereal Library 2013).

Furthermore, Thomas Bradwardine,[10] who lived in the 14th century and was familiar with *The City of God*, characterized five corollaries of God and described God as omnipresent in the first two. First, he stated that *"[...] God is necessarily everywhere in the world and all its parts,"* and second, that God is beyond the real world (Grant 1996, 173f). In addition to these, other opinions exist, and largely result from the Aristotelian cosmos, which is nonexpanding and finite (Grant 1996, xviii), and therefore, contrary to God's omnipresence. However, it is beyond the scope of this book to describe the scientific discussion derived out of the Aristotelian cosmos in detail. For a deeper look into the topic, see the work of Albert Stockl (Stockl 1858).

Over the centuries, God has been described in theology with several adjunctions, which should be considered together. As Wierenga (1989, 1) stated, attributes like supremely wise, powerful, and good derive from different sources and finally lead to broad agreement . Further adjunctions are, among other things, attributes like simplicity, eternality, and incorporeality (Flint and Rea 2009, 213), which are less universal, according to Wierenga (1989). Nevertheless, omniscience, omnipotence, and omnipresence are the classical or traditional attributes of the divine and are often considered together. For Grenz (2000, 92), these attributes were related to God's eternality, whereas Strong (1908, 70) related them to God's creation.

Francks (1979), for example, used both omniscience and omnipotence to describe omnipresence. First, he stated that omniscience is linked with God's complete knowledge[11] in a way that *"[...] it must be true that, for any X, if X is true, then God knows that"* (Francks 1979, 395). In addition to having infinite knowledge, God is characterized as having unlimited power. Second, Francks (1979, 397) stated that God is omnipotent since God can do anything and with comparative ease. Following Francks' argumentation once more, God's infinite knowledge and unlimited power independently lead to the conclusion that God is omnipresent; therefore, God is immanent (1979, 398) or present everywhere.

---

[10] Like St. Anselm, Thomas Bradwardine was Archbishop of Canterbury. Around 1344, he described God's infinite omnipresence in his *In Defense of God against the Pelagians*. Bradwardine died in 1349 (Feingold 2005, 29).

[11] He also said that omniscience requires God's perfect knowledge, but God can still be omniscient without it (Francks 1979, 395).

Moreover, many others also have discussed and interpreted God's omnipresence. In accordance with Francks (1979), McCormick (2000) stated, "*[…] an omnipresent God occupies or is present in all places, far or near, in all times, past, present, or future. His presence does not preclude other things […].*" In contrast to Francks, McCormick considered the time when reflecting omnipresence and additionally pointed out that omnipresence does not mean that anything is precluded. If a divine being is omnipresent at any time and does not exclude anything, "*[…] then there is no place where it is not*" (Dyck 1977, 86). Also, Strong (1907) shared the same opinion. In his book *Systematic Theology*, he stated that God's omnipresence is not a partial omnipresence, but in fact, God as a whole is in any place (1907, 281). He found evidence for this understanding in the Bible.[12] For example, in the Old Testament, Psalm 139:7 states, "*Where can I go from Your Spirit? Or where can I flee from Your presence?*" and Psalm 139:8 reads, "*If I ascend to heaven, You are there; If I make my bed in Sheol, behold, You are there*"[13] (Bible Gateway 1995). Following the same line of logic, omnipresence and corporeality lead to a contradiction in terms because a human being cannot be present anywhere, at any time with no exception. Thus, Dyck (1977, 86) pointed out that omnipresence accompanies incorporeality.

To conclude, Christian theology has a long history of discussing God's omnipresence. However, God is most frequently considered as being present everywhere as well as being incorporeal and all pervading.

2.1.2 Islamic and Hindu Theology

Not only Christian theology discusses and interprets God's omnipresence; in Islamic religion, indications of Allah's omnipresence can be found in the Quran as well. Surah 2:115 states, "*The East and West belong to Allah. Wherever you turn, there is His Face, for Allah is all pervading, all knowing*" (Ahamed 2007, 9). Furthermore, Allah, the God of Islam, is given 99 names in the Quran, which relate to or describes Allah's attributes

---

[12] To improve readability, the 1995 New American Standard Bible is used, which is written in more contemporary English. However, the new version is still based on the American Standard Version from 1901 (Bible Gateway 2013).

[13] In the Hebrew literature, Sheol is described as the underworld, ruled by the god Mot. In contrast, his brother Baal is described as the god of life (Yoeli 1968, 1063).

(Naqvi 2012, 56). In Surah 2:115, Allah is called *Al-'Alim,*[14] or all-knowing (Naqvi 2012, 60). In addition, Allah is described as hidden (Naqvi 2012, 62), which is very similar to Roberts and Donaldson's description of the Christian God as invisible (1870, 385).

In contrast to research on Christianity, just a few journal articles highlight God's omnipresence in Islam. For example, Reid (1916, 13) stated that the doctrine of God's omnipresence dominates Islam and Allah achieves omniscience through omnipresence. Jones (1983, 422) also stated that Allah is omnipresent and omniscient. Finally, Okanmibale (2012, 49) also noted that Allah is considered omnipresent. The same picture emerges from books dealing with Islam, although only a few high-quality books can be found. For example, Freke (2002, 13) mentioned Allah's omnipresence and omnipotence, while King and Brockington (2005, 281) indicated only Allah's omnipresence in time and space.

Finally, based on Surah 2:115, Allah's omnipresence is not limited to certain areas, but is present everywhere, all pervasive, and all knowing (Ahamed 2007, 9). The Quran also provides information that Allah is hidden (Naqvi 2012, 62). No further inferences can be derived since characteristics describing Allah's omnipresence are not discussed in detail in the literature. Allah's omnipresence can be assumed to be similar to God's in the Christian theology, but that assumption cannot be proven through the investigated literature.

Besides Islam, evidences of God's omnipresence also are found in the Hindu religion. Although these evidences are not as concrete as in Christian theology, they are more concrete than in Islam, and can be traced back to the 11th and 12th centuries A.D. As Keene (1953, 3) stated, Ramanuja,[15] a thinker and religious leader of India, developed a *qualified nondualism system,* which can be described in four divisions. One of these is called *salvation,* in which God is described as omnipresent because God's soul is not atomic, and moreover, God has creative power and control over the universe (Keen 1953, 6).

---

[14] *Al-'Alim* is translated as *the knower of all* (Naqvi 2012, 60).
[15] Ramanuja lived between 1055 and 1137. He saw his task as finding a place for the world as well as for the individual, and named his system *qualified nondualism* (Keen 1953, 3).

Furthermore, Swami Sivananda (1998)[16] also described the omnipresence of God in his book *God Exists*. He stated that God, as controller of the universe (1998, 16), is omnipotent, omniscient, and omnipresent. In this context, Sivananda attributed God with absolute knowledge and all-pervading intelligence. Furthermore, he stated that God exists in the past, the present, and the future. Thus, God is temporally independent (1998, 6).

Finally, Thillainathan (2010) showed that God's omnipresence is still a topic of current interest. In *Four Paths to Freedom,* she stated that Hindus consider *"[...] Hinduism as not only a religion, but also a way of life"* (2010, 73). Therefore, according to Sivananda (1998), God is a formless omnipresent and omniscient being that, for an ordinary human intellect, cannot be understood (Thillainathan 2010, 73). However, Thillainathan did not describe God as being present everywhere, but mentioned that human beings can choose their own paths to God (73).

Finally, God's omnipresence is not discussed as much in Islamic and Hindu theologies as in Christian. However, in Hindu theology, God is most often considered to be present everywhere, incorporeal, and all pervading, and in Islamic theology, Allah is most frequently characterized as having immediate and localized knowledge.

2.2 Ubiquity in the Research Field of Law

As highlighted in subchapter 2.1, God's ubiquity or omnipresence, the theological term, is deeply rooted in Christianity, Islam, and Hinduism. However, the term *ubiquity* is used in other fields, too. This chapter explores the field of law and how ubiquity occurs in jurisprudence. The phenomenon of *legal ubiquity* is introduced as well as the *principle of ubiquity*. The legal ubiquity is closely related to ubiquity in theology; however, this book is only an introduction to these concepts, and deeply legal discussions are beyond its scope.

---

[16] Swami Sivananda was born in Pattamadai (Southern India) in 1887 (Venkatesan 2006, 79). He founded the *Divine Life Society*, a spiritual organization, which also impacted Germany, as Boris Sacharow, a disciple of Sivananda, founded the first yoga school in Germany (Strauss 2002).

The term *legal ubiquity* occurs in common law[17] and is closely related to the body of Christ. Over time, Christianity evolved an understanding of Christ's two bodies: the *corpus naturale* seen on the altar and the *corpus mysticum* or the church's administrative structures (Stanford Encyclopedia of Philosophy 2010). Medievalist Ernst Kantorowicz (1957) adapted this dual concept in his book *The King's Two Bodies,* which compares the king's two bodies to Christ's. He states that the king is both mortal and immortal because he has a natural body and also embodies the commonwealth (Smalley 1961, 30).

With this knowledge it is possible to understand what Blackstone (1765, 260)[18] calls *legal ubiquity of the king.* Based on the fact that the king immortal body can legally can never die, he "*[...] acts in a superior sphere*" (Blackstone 1979, 390f). "*His majesty, in the eye of the law, is always present in all his courts [...]*" (Blackstone 1765, 260) and therefore, reaches legal ubiquity. Similar to the majority of theological authors (see Table 1), ubiquity is used in common law to mean being present in any court. The king, who is considered godlike, is always present in all courts, as God is considered to be present everywhere in and outside the real world. However, the king's legal ubiquity was a temporary phenomenon, and in the 18th century, the legal world became very difficult (Helmholz 1990, 1214; Goldberg 2005, 545). Common law is rooted in medieval thinking (Goldberg 2005, 532), in which the king was considered to have both unique personal liberties and unlimited power (Goldberg 2005, 534). Those attributes explain why Blackstone emphasized the king's omnipresence in all courts. Nevertheless, at that time England was Protestant and already had cut the ties with the medieval conception of the world (Helmholz 1990, 1214). Therefore, common lawyers like William Blackstone began to focus on defining Englishmen's rights and liberties (Helmholz 1990, 1214; Goldberg 2005, 532) with such statements as "*[...] disputes about the prerogative rights and powers of the Crown [...]*" (Helmholz 1990, 1215). Additionally, they demanded no interference with their operation and required the au-

---

[17] "*In a common law legal system, such as that of the United States and the United Kingdom, many important laws are made not by legislatures but by appellate courts deciding specific cases and therefore, creating precedents*" (Gennaioli and Shleifer 2007, 43).

[18] William Blackstone was born in 1723 in London (Odgers 1918, 612). His *Commentaries on the Laws of England* influenced common law in Great Britain in the 18th century since he summarized and explained political thoughts of the last centuries (Kantorowicz 1997, 4).

tonomy of courts (Goldberg 2005, 539). Therefore, legal ubiquity as described was a transitional phase between common law from the Middle Ages and the separation from political and moral influences of jurisprudence that occurred in the 19th century (Berman 1994, 1736). Legal ubiquity is no longer relevant.

In addition to the king's legal ubiquity, the *principle of ubiquity* (*Ubiquitätsprinzip*) can be found in the German law as well. According to article 40 (1) of the German Civil Code, *"Tort claims are governed by the law of the country in which the liable party has acted. The injured party can demand that instead of this law, the law of the country in which the injury occurred is to be applied"* (Juris 2012). Therefore, in principle for distance torts, such as shots across the border or false credit information within international trade, the law of the place where the injury occurred is applied, unless the injured party wants to apply the law of that place where the damaging result occurred (Kropholler 2006, 524).[19]

As a result, in contrast to legal ubiquity, which considers the king to be present in any court, the principle of ubiquity links a different place with the place where an injury occurred. In the end, two laws can be considered for one tort. Thus, the principle of ubiquity is a figure of speech while legal ubiquity is a temporary phenomenon.

However, both legal ubiquity and the principle of ubiquity are no longer considered. First, the principle of ubiquity is a legal construct limited to only two places. Furthermore, ubiquity in this area is strictly regulated by law that provide the opportunity to assign one or the other place to an object instead of actually transferring the object to a place. Second, legal ubiquity no longer has any significance in modern jurisprudence because the monarch's strong influence, especially in England, ended with the Bill of Rights[20] in the late 17th century (Hartmann 2011, 52). Until then, legal ubiquity was used to defend the crown's privileges, which in modern times are almost obsolete.

---

[19] The principle of ubiquity can be found in the German Criminal Code (§ 9) as well. Further information, including detailed descriptions and examples, are presented in the German book *Europäisches Strafrecht* (Hecker 2012, 30ff).

[20] The Bill of Rights Ordinance ensures first that the Parliament is convened regularly, and second, that it is involved in the legislation process and is independent of the judiciary committee. King William III was the first monarch to take the oath on the Bill of Rights, which finally embedded the constitutional monarchy as form of government in England. Even though the crown still has a veto right on decisions of Parliament, monarchs have not used this right since the early 18th century (Hartmann 2011, 51ff).

However, legal ubiquity, which is closely related to God's omnipresence, can strengthen the importance of this characterization even though it is no longer relevant.

2.3 Identified Characteristics of Ubiquity in the Research Field of Humanities

As the etymology discussion in Chapter 2 indicates, ubiquity in theology means being present everywhere, and in fact, being timely independent (Harper 2010; Dictionary.com 2013). This chapter builds on the results and findings from subchapter 2.1 and subchapter 2.2 to identify characteristics for ubiquity. In the later part of this book (see subchapter 5.3), these findings are used to define ubiquity in scientific entrepreneurship.

Subchapter 2.1 took a deeper look into Christian theology, which is very present in Europe with about 558 million Christians, and in North America with about 227 million (Pew Research Center's Forum on Religion and Public Life 2012b). Because of the wide distribution of Christian theology, we can presume that the literature will include the topic in detail and will be widely available in Europe and the US. Therefore, several articles were identified to explain ubiquity in Christian theology.

Fewer scientific articles were found in to describe ubiquity in Islam and Hinduism, perhaps because these religions are less prominent in Europe and North America. However, similarities were identified among these religions. Table 1 summarizes characteristics of ubiquity derived from the listed theological interpretations, namely being present everywhere, being incorporeal and all pervading, having immediate and localized knowledge, being invisible, and not precluding anything. For each religion, the identified sources are cited and assigned to the derived characteristics.

Table 1: Analysis of characteristics of ubiquity in theology (Source: Own representation)

Interpretations		Characteristics				
		Present every where	Incorporeal and all-pervading	Immediate and localized knowledge	Invisible	Not precluding anything
	"[…] If a being is omnipresent, then there is no place where it is not" (Dyck 1977, 86).	X	X			
	Omnipresence "[…] is ultimately reducible to a kind of knowledge, immediate and localized for every region" (Flint and Rea 2009, 201).			X		
	"God's will is omnipresent, or every point in space is a point at which God's will is continually in operation" (Francks 1979, 398). Francks also stated that God's omnipresence is derived from Its infinite knowledge (395).	X	X	X		
	"[…] God is necessarily everywhere in the world and all its parts […] and also beyond the real world […]" (Grant 1996, 173).	X	X			
	"[…] All things are seen and heard [by God] […]" (Lightfoot 1889, 286).	X				
	"[…] An omnipresent God occupies or is present in all places, far or near, in all times, past, present, or future. His presence does not preclude other things […]" (McCormick 2000).	X	X			X
	"[…] God is in the bottomless depths, and exists everywhere […] [and] the Son, being indivisible from Him, is everywhere with Him" (Roberts and Donaldson 1870, 385).	X	X		X	
	God "[…] who is wholly everywhere, included in no space, bound by no chains, mutable in no part of His being, [is] filling heaven and earth with omnipresent power […]" (Schaff 2007, 140).	X	X			
Christianity	"God's omnipresence is not the presence of a part but of the whole of God in every place [sic.]. This follows from the conception of God as incorporeal" (Strong 1907, 281).	X	X			
Islam	"The East and West belong to Allah. Wherever you turn, there is His Face, for Allah is all pervading, all knowing" (Ahamed 2007, 9)	X	X	X		
	Allah is, inter alia, called Al-'Alim, which			X	X	

	Characteristics				
Interpretations	Present every where	Incorporeal and all-pervading	Immediate and localized knowledge	Invisible	Not precluding anything
attributes Him as all knowing (Naqvi 2012, 60) and besides, He is described as hidden (Naqvi 2012, 62)					
"[...] God is omnipresent, while individual soul is atomic [...]" (Keen 1953, 6)	X	X			
"God is [...] Knowledge Absolute [...]. God is all-pervading intelligence or consciousness. [...] He exists [sic.] *past, present and future"* (Sivananda 1998, 6).	X	X	X		
"It must be noted that God in Hinduism is a formless omnipresent, omniscient being that cannot be comprehended by the ordinary human intellect" (Thillainathan 2010, 73).				X	
Total	**11**	**10**	**5**	**3**	**1**

(Left margin label: Hinduism)

As the table shows, a total of five characteristics can be derived. Across all investigated religions, God is most frequently considered to be present everywhere. The second most frequent characteristic is incorporeal or all pervading, followed by all knowing, which puts God in a position to have immediate and localized knowledge from anywhere. In comparison with the other two religions, only Christianity considers God as not precluding anything.

This conclusion is based on a basic set of 14 sources, which described these five characteristics of God in the three religions 30 times. Thus, each source assigned approximately two characteristics to God. As mentioned, Christian literature dominates these statistics: nine out of 14 sources described the Christian God, while two sources described the Islamic God, and three the Hindu God. Based on Table 1, Figure 2 graphically represents the distribution of characteristics per religion, mainly influenced by the Christian literature.

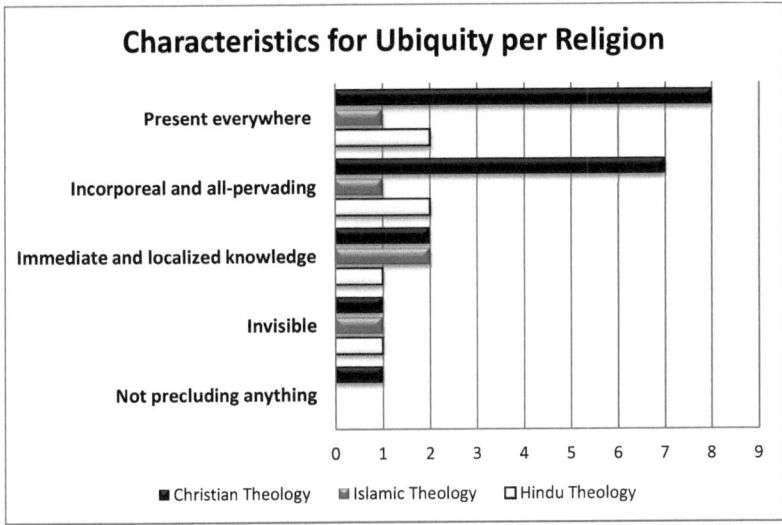

Figure 2: Distribution of ubiquity's characteristics per religion. (Source: Own representation.)

Finally, Lightfoot (1889, 286) stated that God sees and hears all things, a statement that can be interpreted to mean that God is present everywhere, which is a prerequisite for seeing and hearing everything. Furthermore, Naqvi (2012, 62) described God as hidden, which can be interpreted as being invisible.

Subchapter 2.2 analyzed how ubiquity is interpreted in the field of law. To summarize, legal ubiquity attributes godlike characteristics to the king, and makes him present in every court. However, legal ubiquity is a temporary phenomenon and is no longer relevant in modern times. In addition, the principle of ubiquity is a virtual construct for jurisprudence in which the term *ubiquity* is used as only as a figure of speech. Therefore, this book does not consider legal ubiquity or the principle of ubiquity to characterize ubiquity. Nevertheless, legal ubiquity, which states that the king as being present everywhere within the courts, underlines the importance of the first characteristic derived from theology, namely that God is present everywhere.

Therefore, the following conclusion can be drawn: God's ubiquity plays an important role in theology since God is described as being present everywhere in almost all circumstances (with no area where God is not), in all times (including past, present and future), and God does not preclude anything and is reducible to knowledge. However, being present everywhere and being all pervading are by far the most frequently used attributes.[21]

---

[21] Refer to subchapter 5.3, where these characteristics are utilized to define ubiquity in the field of scientific entrepreneurship.

3 Ubiquity in the Research Field of Information Technology

Supplementary to Chapter 2, which discuss omnipresence through history, ubiquity also plays a major role in modern times, especially in ubiquitous computing, which already carries ubiquity in its name. However, according to Lyytinen and Yoo (2002, 63), a distinction must be made between ubiquitous computing and mobile and pervasive computing, which often are used interchangeably. They propose a two-dimensional framework in which the level of mobility serves as the horizontal axis and the level of embeddedness as the vertical (64). As Figure 3 shows, traditional business computing has a low level of embeddedness combined with a low level of mobility because it aims to lower knowledge barriers within an organizational network (cf. Attewell 1992, 16) and to extract knowledge (Desikan et al. 2009, 45) while using traditional computing devices.

The same level of embeddedness but a higher level of mobility leads to mobile computing. Mobile computing focuses not only on an organizational network but also on the World Wide Web. Hence, adding mobility to Web computing leads to mobile computing (Saha et al. 2003, 4), which increases the capability of devices to be physically moved, making them ever present, location independent, and communicating (Lyytinen and Yoo 2002, 63). In addition, the digital world can be accessed regardless of what (mobile) device is used, and therefore, mobile computing is a step toward making computers "disappearing," with an "anytime and anywhere" goal (Saha and Mukherjee 2003, 26). However, mobile computing is limited by its own model, which does not allow context awareness because devices cannot flexibly obtain information about the environment and adjust accordingly (Lyytinen and Yoo 2002, 64). With an increase in the embeddedness, pervasive computing can be achieved, where intelligent computers use available information from their environments. However, Saha and Mukherjee (2003, 26) describe the "all the time everywhere" goal of pervasive computing as a superset of mobile computing, supporting "[...] interoperability, scala-

bility, smartness, and invisibility to ensure that users have seamless access to compu-ting whenever they need it."

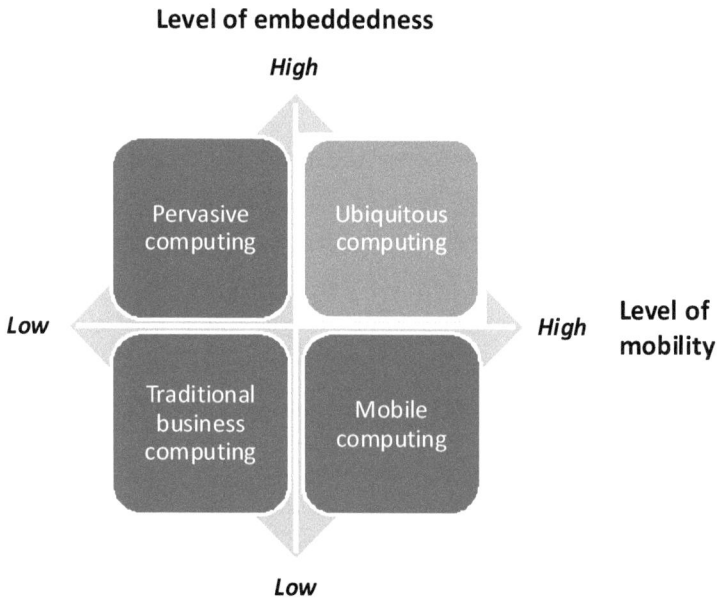

Figure 3: Dimensions for ubiquitous computing.
(Source: Own representation based on Lyytinen and Yoo [2002, 64].)

Although pervasive computing has a low level of mobility, ubiquitous computing *"[in] its ultimate form [...] means any computing device, while moving with us, can build incrementally dynamic models of its various environments and configure its services accordingly"* (Lyytinen and Yoo 2002, 64).

Subchapter 3.1 describes ubiquitous computing in detail, starting with the early begin-ning in the late 1980s (see 3.1.1) and ending with the current state of research in the 21st century (see 3.1.2), and focusing on the exploratory identification of characteris-tics of ubiquity in IT. Subchapter 3.2 analyzes these identified characteristics in tabular form.

3.1 Ubiquitous Computing

Without Mark Weiser,[22] research in ubiquitous computing would not be where it is today. From the beginning, Weiser was the driving force to promote the idea of ubiquitous computing adapted to human environments, and according to his vision that *"[...] using a computer [is] as refreshing as taking a walk in the woods"* (1991, 104). Subchapter 3.1.1 describes the history of ubiquitous computing and Weiser's visionary thoughts. The current state of research is presented in 3.1.2 and Weiser's vision is developed further.

3.1.1 The Early Development of Ubiquitous Computing

In the late 1980s, the Electronics and Imaging Laboratory (EIL) of the Xerox Palo Alto Research Center (PARC) *"[...] proposed fabricating large, wall-sized, flat-panel computer displays"* (Weiser et al. 1999, 693). The vision of "computer walls" surpassed the "one computer for one person" paradigm, with an idea to ubiquitously and invisibly spread computers throughout the environment (Weiser et al. 1999, 693). Afterwards, a ubiquitous computing program emerged at PARC that sought to move beyond the isolation, complexity, and domination of desktop computers, to create a new field of computer science in which computers would be seamlessly embedded in the physical world using sensors,[23] continuous networks, and other computational elements (Weiser et al. 1999, 693f).

Among all the PARC researchers, Mark Weiser was the father of ubiquitous computing, who first described it in the article *The Computer for the 21st Century,* which highlighted the idea that one person uses many computers (1991). Weiser's envisioned computers that would take the natural human environment into account and invisibly enhance the world in the background (1991, 94). Furthermore, he described computers interconnected in a ubiquitous network (96) and, most important, that would overcome information overload (104). Hence, Weiser's vision planted *"[...] the seed for a*

---

[22] Mark Weiser was born in 1952 and died of cancer in 1999. He was an entrepreneur who started two companies the early 1970s. In 1987, Weiser joined the Xerox Palo Alto Research Center (PARC). Furthermore, Mark Weiser was the drummer of the rock band "Severe Tire Damage," the first band to play live on the Internet (Weiser et al. 1999, 695).

[23] As discussed in 3.1.2, Weiser talked about context awareness, but he never explicitly mentioned that sensors and other elements are used to achieve context awareness.

new paradigm in computing that is arguably set to dominate the coming decades" (Galloway 2004, 385).

Two years later, Mark Weiser published another article in which he again highlighted the importance of using natural interfaces to integrate computers invisibly into the user's environment (1993). However, he described the solution to information over-load in more detail, with computers as autonomous agents taking on users' goals (76). He introduced three computers of different sizes, which he called boards, pads, and tabs, that would be frequently available to any person. Phase one of ubiquitous com-puting starts *"[...] to construct, deploy, and learn from a computing environment con-sisting of tabs, pads, and boards"* (76). He also was aware that ubiquitous computing requires a mobile cellular network that these devices could use permanently (79). Con-sidered against the background of the German today, Weiser's thoughts are indeed visionary. He described his vision in detail during a time when the German mobile phone industry was a duopoly, ruled by T-Mobil and Mannesmann Mobilfunk (Grimm et al. 2003, 1560) and data services like the short message service (SMS) were just be-ginning to become popular.

However, as in his first article, Weiser was aware of privacy issues associated with ubiquitous computing, and he stated that it *"[...] is important to realize there can never be a purely technological solution to privacy, and social issues must be considered [...]"* (1993, 82). Therefore, instead of describing only what ubiquitous computing can do, Weiser also describes what ubiquitous computing is not (Galloway 2004, 386) or can-not do.

Weiser characterized ubiquitous computing as being invisible and collaborating, as machines interact. Furthermore, he indicated that context awareness plays a major role in ubiquitous computing. The greatest barrier to ubiquitous computing's success is privacy protection.

3.1.2 Ubiquitous Computing in the 21st Century

This subchapter describes how ubiquitous computing developed and how other researchers built upon Weiser's vision following his death in 1999. However, technical solutions are not the focus here.

In 2000, Abowd and Mynatt developed the idea that natural interfaces can enrich the variety of communications between humans and computers, and furthermore, that context-aware applications can adapt information from the environment (2000, 30). For them, natural human forms of user interfaces increase communication with the device allowing the device to better support users' tasks (32). As indicated, Abowd and Mynatt explicitly mentioned context awareness for ubiquitous computing in detail. They stated, *"[…] a complete definition of context is illusive, [but] the 'five W's' of context are a good minimal set of necessary context"* (2000, 37). Bravo et al. (2005, 1497) also pointed out that *context* is comprehensively described in many studies; they referred to the *five Ws* (who, what, where, when, and why), which Brooks (2003) called *content quintet,* and Abowd and Mynatt (2000, 37) described as the *five Ws.*

Table 2 depicts a comparison of these two views of context awareness that Abowd and Mynatt and Brooks described.

Table 2: Comparing context awareness. (Source: Own representation.)

Context awareness	Five Ws (Abowd and Mynatt 2000)	Content quintet (Brooks 2003)
Who?	Human activities are based on past events and the presence of other people.	Determining *identity awareness* is difficult since it implies that a complex construct of frequently changing relationships must be managed.
What?	Human activities are interpreted, and relevant information is usefully provided.	Knowing what task a user performs leads to *task awareness* so that devices are able to recognize these task patterns and finally semiautonomously perform them.

Context awareness	Five Ws (Abowd and Mynatt 2000)	Content quintet (Brooks 2003)
Where?	This component requires additional exploration, but combinations with temporal information are of particular interest.	*Location awareness* determines experiences, which can be used to deduce the location's meaning to the user.
When?	Temporal information is used to interpret and understand human activities.	Knowing time and date information creates a *temporal awareness*, fundamental to a time-dependent culture.
Why?	The combination of other context aware information can be used to understand why a person is doing certain things.	Why is the hardest question of all, and confidence increases if the user knows why a device performs a particular task.

As shown, identity awareness can be reached if a complex construct of relationships can be determined out of the past to predict current relationships. Thus, identity awareness is closely related to temporal awareness, which is used to interpret time-dependent human actions. Afterwards, task awareness can be used not only to interpret human actions but also to perform these actions autonomously. Time awareness and task awareness can be complemented with location awareness to interpret where a user performs a specific task during a certain time. Finally, the reasons for a using doing certain things must be determined.

In this book, context awareness is described as outlined in Table 2, although the term can be explained in far more detail, too. For example, Prekop and Burnett (2003) analyzed context awareness through an activity-centric view, or that which surrounds an activity performed by an agent. Also, Anagnostopoulos et al. (2007) described software architectures for context awareness. These different approaches to context awareness are beyond the scope of this book, but the latter two sources are recommended for further readings.

Mattern (2001, 1) described ubiquitous computing from a technological point of view, stating what remains to be connected to the Internet to provide information task, temporal, and location awareness. Compared with Abowd and Mynatt (2000) and Brooks (2003), Mattern focused on the technical view and did not consider the "why" an "who" questions. Mattern also highlighted that short-range communication for ubiquitous computing is extremely relevant, which leads to enormous challenges in privacy because a clear distinction between online and offline can no longer be made (2001, 3). Clearly, privacy issues have moved into focus. What Weiser (1991, 104) 10 years earlier called key among all social issues has become a key discussion. As a result, additional articles have addressed privacy issues. For example, in *The Future of Business Services in the Age of Ubiquitous Computing,* Fano and Gershman (2002) stated that privacy is an increasingly important concern, arguing that new business opportunities for privacy management are created because *"[i]f we value privacy, someone will sell it to us"* (87). They took the view that privacy issues can be overcome relatively easily. In contrast, Lyytinen et al. (2004, 702) identified major impacts on user privacy, and Hong and Landay (2004, 177) pointed out that *"[p]rivacy is the most often-cited criticism of ubiquitous computing, and may be the greatest barrier to its long-term success."*

Finally, the role of trust is a subject for analysis in the field of ubiquitous computing. Langheinrich (2003, 3) discovered that trust in ubiquitous computing is mostly related to the expansion of network security's trust concepts. On the one hand, the concept of trust is too complex for one definition as a starting point; on the other hand, a more complex framework will *"[...] end up with so many variables that could potentially affect a single trust decision"* (2003, 4) that recommendations seem to be impossible. Hence, Langheinrich concluded that trust assessments in the field of ubiquitous computing should be left up to humans (2003, 1).

In summary, the development of the characteristics of ubiquitous computing has progressed beyond Weiser's thoughts to focus on context awareness, describing it with the five Ws (Table 2). In addition, trustworthiness in the 21st century is also under consideration in the characterization of ubiquitous computing.

3.2 Identified Characteristics of Ubiquity in the Research Field of Information Technology

Ubiquitous computing is technically influenced to achieve high levels of embeddedness and mobility (Lyytinen and Yoo 2002, 64). Subchapter 3.1 analyzed the development of ubiquitous computing focusing on how ubiquity is described. Of course, far more articles are available in the area of ubiquitous computing, but only 14 articles were identified that directly discussed ubiquity. As shown in Table 3, the characteristics of ubiquity within IT can be derived from these 14 articles, namely context aware, privacy protecting, collaborating, invisible, and trustworthy. The identified sources are cited so that they can be assigned to the derived characteristics.

Table 3: Analysis of characteristics of ubiquity in ubiquitous computing. (Source: Own representation.)

Interpretations	Characteristics				
	Context aware	Privacy protecting	Collaborating	Invisible	Trustworthy
"In addition to showing some of the ways that computers can find their way invisibly into people's lives, this speculation points up some of the social issues that embodied virtuality will engender. Perhaps key among them is privacy [...]" (Weiser 1991, 104).		X		X	
"These machines and more will be interconnected in a ubiquitous network" (Weiser 1991, 96).			X		
Ubiquitous computing "[...] created a new field of computer science, one that speculated on a physical world richly and invisibly interwoven with sensors, actuators, displays, and computational elements, embedded seamlessly in the everyday objects of our lives and connected through a continuous network" (Weiser et al. 1999, 694).	X		X	X	
"So a key problem with ubiquitous computing is preserving privacy" (Weiser 1993, 82).		X			
Ubiquitous computing is a "[...] next-generation computing environment in which each person is continually with hundreds of nearby wirelessly interconnected computers [...] [who are] invisible to the user" (Weiser 1993, 75).			X	X	
"We desire natural interfaces that facilitate a		X			

Interpretations	Characteristics				
	Context aware	Privacy protecting	Collaborating	Invisible	Trustworthy
richer variety of communications capabilities between humans and computation" (Abowd and Mynatt 2000, 30).					
"Ubicomp [ubiquitous computing] applications need to be context aware, adapting their behavior based on information sensed from the physical and computational environment" (Abowd and Mynatt 2000, 30).	X				
"The real goal for ubicomp [ubiquitous computing] is to provide many single-activity interactions that together promote a unified and continuous interaction between humans and computational services" (Abowd and Mynatt 2000, 53)			X		
"In Ubiquitous Computing [...] context-aware applications are obtained" (Bravo et al. 2005, 1494). Furthermore, the article's chapter three explains context-awareness in detail (Bravo et al. 2005, 1497).	X				
"A growing research activity within ubiquitous computing deals with the challenges of context-aware computing" (Dey et al. 2001, 100).	X				
"[...] [U]sing context to tag captured information may at first seem like an intrusion to individual privacy" (Dey et al. 2001, 158)		X			
"From a technological point of view, one could describe 'ubiquitous computing' as the prospect of connecting the remaining things in the world to the Internet, in order to provide information 'on anything, anytime, anywhere.' [sic] Putting it in another way, the term 'ubiquitous computing' signifies the omnipresence of tiny, wirelessly interconnected computers that are embedded almost invisibly into just about any kind of everyday object" (Mattern 2001, 1).	X		X	X	
"If the age of ubiquitous computing extends the Internet into everyday objects, this alone will result in enormous challenges for our privacy [...]" (Mattern, 2001, p. 3)		X			
"The potential scenario of sensors in your bathroom and mobile devices reporting your every move to remote service providers naturally inspires grave privacy concerns" (Fano and Gershman 2002, 87).		X			

	Characteristics				
Interpretations	Context aware	Privacy protecting	Collaborating	Invisible	Trustworthy
"*Ubiquitous computing applications should be both context and location-aware [...]*" (Lyytinen et al. 2004, 700).	X				
"*One major impact of ubiquitous computing is on user privacy*" (Lyytinen et al. 2004, 702).		X			
"*Privacy is the most often-cited criticism of ubiquitous computing, and may be the greatest barrier to its long-term success*" (Hong and Landay 2004, 177).		X			
"*[...] [C]ontext-awareness provides computing environments with the ability to usefully adapt the services or information they provide*" (Prekop and Burnett 2003, 1168).	X				
"*[...] [U]biquitous computing is currently seen to comprise [...] context-aware computing applications*" (Galloway 2004, 388).	X				
"*To achieve such a persistent collaboration throughout the supply chain, a ubiquitous infrastructure and middleware is necessary*" (Strassner and Schoch 2002, 73).			X		
"*However, even though trust-based access control is gaining momentum in the field of ubiquitous computing, much remains unclear when it comes to defining the problem [author's note: the role of trust in ubiquitous computing] we are trying to solve*" (Langheinrich 2003, 2).					X
Total	8	7	7	4	1

As shown in the table above, five characteristics were derived from the investigated sources that describe ubiquity in the field of ubiquitous computing. Context awareness was the most frequent characteristic, closely followed by privacy protection and collaboration. Invisibly was mentioned fourth often, and trustworthiness ranked last with just one reference.

The five derived characteristics were mentioned 27 times in total, or each characteristic was mentioned approximately twice per source. Based on Table 3, Figure 4 graphically represents the distribution of characteristics of ubiquity in information technology.

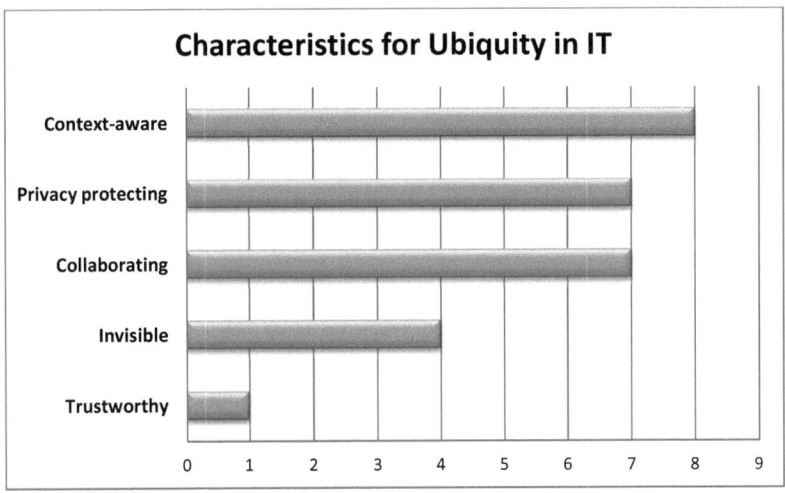

Figure 4: Distribution of characteristics of ubiquity in IT. (Source: Own representation.)

In the scope of this book, context awareness is, accordingly to Table 2, refers to the content quintet (Brooks 2003) or the five Ws (Abowd and Mynatt 2000), even though it is not consistently described that way in literature. Weiser (1999, 694), for example, does not mention context awareness at all but describes it as a network interwoven with sensors. Nevertheless according to Galloway (2004, 388), this statement can be interpreted as context awareness. For reasons of comparability, context awareness is always interpreted according to Brooks (2003) and Abowd and Mynatt (2000). Furthermore, privacy protection is often highlighted as the greatest barrier to ubiquity in IT. Conversely, it is one of the most important characteristics to reach ubiquity. Therefore, this attribute is used to characterize ubiquity, too.

Finally, one additional remark should be made with regarding the attribute *"collaborating."* An analysis of the references describing collaboration seems to indicate that the authors emphasized interconnection (Weiser 1991; Weiser 1993; Weiser et al.

1999; Mattern 2001) and interaction (Abowd and Mynatt 2000), respectively. However, these references are characterized as collaborating because modern technology can easily identify people or objects without any user interaction (Bravo et al. 2005, 1496). Nevertheless, without collaboration the identified context would be considered isolated and context awareness, which highly influences ubiquity, could not be reached. Hence, interconnections as well as interactions must be included in collaboration.

To sum up, the following conclusion can be drawn: Ubiquity in IT is characterized as being context aware (described here according to Table 2), in which privacy protection is essential. Furthermore, ubiquity is described as collaborating, but also as invisible and trustworthy.[24]

---

[24] Refer to subchapter 5.3, where these characteristics are utilized in combination with the characteristics from subchapter 2.3 to describe ubiquitous entrepreneurship.

4 Entrepreneurship

Entrepreneurship is a wide-ranging research field, where *the* definition does not exist (cf. Gartner 1990; Bruyat and Julien 2000; Anderson and Starnawska 2008). To understand how entrepreneurship has developed, a glance back at history is helpful. For example, Hoselitz (1960) analyzed the early history of entrepreneurship. According to him, the earliest French meaning was formed during the Middle Ages and can be found in the *Dictionnaire de la langue française* written by Émile Littré[25] (1960, 235). In the second volume an entrepreneur is described as *"[c]elui, celle qui entreprend quelque chose"* (Littré 1863, 1437), or a person who does something. During the Middle Ages an entrepreneur typically was a cleric in charge when religious buildings were planned and constructed or when workers need to be hired and managed (Hoselitz 1960, 237). However, during this time entrepreneurs bore no risks because they were not responsible for completing a project successfully (Hoselitz 1960, 237). After the Middle Ages, religious buildings declined in importance, and secular public buildings become more prominent, requiring new entrepreneurial skills like material procurement or wage negotiations. Therefore, the entrepreneur, finally, needed know the revenues and expenditures in order to minimize his costs and achieve profit maximization (Hoselitz 1960, 239). In Hoselitz's analysis, the English word *undertaker*, especially in the 17th century, was a common equivalent for the French word *entrepreneur, and* the undertaker's historical development was similar to the French entrepreneurs' (Hoselitz 1960, 240).

Hoselitz (1960) describes the early history of entrepreneurship is in far more detail, and the work is highly recommended for further readings. However, a detailed summary is beyond the scope of this book. Instead, subchapter 4.1 briefly explains the most common theories of entrepreneurship and also shows that entrepreneurship means different things to different people. Moreover, the lack of a uniform definition for entrepreneurship is introduced in subchapter 4.1. Therefore, subchapter 4.2 theoretically categorizes entrepreneurship, focusing on three spheres that Cuevas (1994)

---

[25] The positivist Littré (1801–1881) wrote the French dictionary, *Dictionnaire de la langue française,* in four volumes between 1863 and 1873 (Encyclopædia Britannica 2013).

identified to describe entrepreneurship: the booster sphere, financial sphere, and management sphere. This approach allows a holistic view of entrepreneurship. Finally, subchapter 4.3 summarizes why entrepreneurship is important in today and why it is promoted.

4.1 Entrepreneurship Theories

"Entrepreneurship is a multifaceted phenomenon that cuts across many disciplinary boundaries. Studies falling under the rubric of 'entrepreneurship' have pursued a wide range of purposes and objectives, asked different questions, and adopted different units of analysis, theoretical perspectives, and methodologies" (Low and MacMillan 1988, 140). As Low and MacMillan's statement indicates, several entrepreneurship theories exist. The first to who describe entrepreneurship was Richard Cantillon[26] (Hoselitz 1960, 235; Hébert and Link 1989, 41; Stevenson and Jarillo 1990, 18; Wennekers and Thurik 1999, 31). According to Hébert and Link (1989) and Cuevas (1994), Cantillon identified three economic agents: the financially independent land-owner; the profit-oriented entrepreneur, who takes the risk while engaging in market exchanges; and finally, the stable, income-fixed hireling, who avoids active decision making (Hébert and Link 1989, 42; Cuevas 1994, 79). Cantillon described the entrepreneur as a person who buys something at a certain price, but sells it at an uncertain price (Hoselitz 1960, 240; Hébert and Link 1989, 42; Stevenson and Jarillo 1990, 18). Therefore, the entrepreneur assumes a risk to make profits (Bruyat and Julien 2000, 167) since his total income is uncertain (Hoselitz 1960, 240). Finally, Hébert and Link (1989) noted that Cantillon emphasized the entrepreneur's function and not his personality, and, moreover, removed the entrepreneur from the social status so that even a robber could be seen as entrepreneurs because the robber also faces economic uncertainty (Hébert and Link 1989, 42).

---

[26] Cantillon, who was born in 1697, had a mysterious life and was murdered in 1734 by his former cook. He wrote the *Essai Sur La Nature du Commerce en Général* (Essay on the Nature of Trade in General) between 1730 and 1734, which was published entirely in 1755 (Spengler 1954).

Besides Cantillon's theory, three other major theories can be found. The first is the so-called German tradition, characterized by Johann Heinrich von Thünen[27] and Joseph Alois Schumpeter.[28] In *The Isolated State*, Thünen theoretically described a special business scenario, and identified *"[...] entrepreneurial gain as profit minus (1) interest on invested capital, (2) insurance against business losses, and (3) the wages of management"* (Hébert and Link 2006, 592). Furthermore, he highlighted that the entrepreneur must take a certain risk, but also must be an innovator (Formaini 2001, 5). Schumpeter developed the theory that the entrepreneur's innovation leads to a creative response to economic change (Frank 1998, 505). Similar to Cantillon, Schumpeter described the entrepreneur as an innovator able to change the economy (Bruyat and Julien 2000, 167) by implementing new combinations, which causes discontinuity (Bull and Willard 1993, 186). Furthermore, Schumpeter argued that entrepreneurship is the process *"[...] by which the economy as a whole goes forward"* (Stevenson and Jarillo 1990, 18). He viewed the entrepreneur as the *persona causa* in economic development (Hébert and Link 1989, 43), which is associated with innovation (Stevenson and Jarillo 1990, 19).

Second, Frank Knight[29] and Theodore Schultz[30] comprise the Chicago tradition. Knight (1942) described the entrepreneur as a specialist able to take risks and to bear uncertainty (Knight 1942, 129). As Hébert and Link (1989, 43) stated, Knight was the first to distinguish between risk and uncertainty. While some forms of risks can be insured, *"[u]ncertainty is a pervasive fact of everyday life"* (Hébert and Link 1989, 43) that the entrepreneur must deal with. According to Schultz (1980, 437), entrepreneurship is an activity in dynamic economies, in which entrepreneurs must deal with disequilibria occurring in market and nonmarket activities (Schultz 1975, 829). Schultz (1980, 439) also highlighted that entrepreneurship leads to economic value, *"[...] which implies*

---

[27] Thünen (1783–1850) is described as loner and mastermind. In 1826, he wrote *The Isolated State*, based on the first ideas he had in 1803 when he was still a minor (Samuelson 1983, 1468).

[28] Schumpeter was born in Austria in 1883, went to Harvard before Hitler came to power, and died in Taconic, Connecticut in 1950 (Giersch 1984, 103).

[29] Frank Night lived between 1885 and 1972, received his Ph.D. in economics, but is also considered social philosopher (Hausman 1994, 111).

[30] Schultz was born in South Dakota in 1902 and died shortly after his 96th birthday in 1998. In 1979, he and Arthur Lewis were awarded with the Nobel Prize in economics (Nerlove 1999, F726).

that there is a supply and a demand for their services." Stationary economies with economic equilibrium, Schultz (1980, 441) argued, do not need entrepreneurs until economic disequilibria arise, which mostly come along with economic growth. Finally, he concluded that experiences and education could enhance entrepreneurship (Schultz 1980, 448).

Third, the (modern) Austrian tradition, influenced by Ludwig von Mises[31] and Israel Kirzner,[32] includes theories focusing on a financial perspective. Von Mises (1946, 60) stated that every entrepreneur has a profit motive in which either costs are lowered or products are improved (Von Mises 1946, 68). Furthermore, he stated that *"[...] an entrepreneur who does not calculate [...] would very soon go bankrupt [...]"* (29) since entrepreneurs will not invest in projects without the prospect of profitability (25). Similar to Schultz (1980), he maintained that stable prices do not offer any room for entrepreneurial activities, but within a permanently changing world, continuous adjustment is required, and at this point the entrepreneur emerges (28). Kirzner was a student of von Mises and was influenced by him. Thus, Kirzner (1997, 69) stated that in equilibrium the entrepreneur has nothing to do since profit cannot be made. The pure entrepreneurial profit, Kirzner (1997, 69) argued, is *"[...] created by temporary absence of full adjustment between input and output markets [...]."* Finally, he summarized that the entrepreneur is responsible for the market's ever-changing process since each market (except the one with complete equilibrium) offers opportunities for pure entrepreneurial profit (70).

Moreover, further entrepreneurial theories can be found. For example, Leibenstein[33] was a representative of the noneconomic tradition (Cuevas 1994, 78), who viewed the entrepreneur as *"gap-filler,"* *"input-completer,"* and *"[...] prime mover of the capacity creation part of [...][the] elements of the [economic] growth process"* (Leibenstein 1968, 77). Therefore, entrepreneurship consists on the one hand of the management-

---

[31] Von Mises, 1881–1973, was an economist highly influenced by Israel Kirzner. Due to his Jewish ancestry, he immigrated to the United States in 1940. One year after von Mises' death, Friedrich Hayek received the Nobel Prize for a theory he pioneered with von Mises (Butler 2010, 9–27).
[32] The economist Kirzner was born in London in 1930 and was a student of Ludwig von Mises. Therefore, Kirzner focused on Austrian economics during his research career (Kirzner 2005, 81).
[33] Harvey Leibenstein was born in 1922 in Russia, received his Ph.D. at Princeton University, and moved to Harvard University in 1967. Leibenstein died in 1994 (Putterman and Kroszner 1996, 267).

oriented and coordinating *routine entrepreneurship,* while on the other hand it requires the *new type entrepreneurship* that creates or carries on enterprises
(Leibenstein 1968, 72). Therefore, Leibenstein (1968, 72) described the entrepreneur
as having a unique and critical role within economics that is significantly important in
the development process because the entrepreneur must coordinate various market
activities (73).

In addition, economists such as Walras[34] or Coase[35] emphasized the management-
oriented entrepreneur (Coase 1937; Walker 1986). Walker (1986, 5) stated that
Walras' theory describes the entrepreneur as someone who supplies productive services and sells products. Eventually, the entrepreneur intervenes in economics when
executing activities, which according to Walras, belong to routine management
(Walker 1986, 5). This description is similar to what Leibenstein (1968, 72) called coordinating routine entrepreneurship. Also Coase (1937, 388) put the entrepreneur in the
role of a coordinator directing the production, when he described him as a *"[...] person
or persons who, in a competitive system, take the place of the price mechanism in the
direction of resources."* He concluded that an entrepreneur carries out management
functions at less cost and forms a system of relationships when directing resources
(392). However, the entrepreneur's central function decreases due to specialization,
Coase (1937, 394) argued, when a firm gets larger.

Summing up, several views were briefly introduced to describe entrepreneurship;
however, this overview makes no claim to be complete because other theories of entrepreneurship exist and these theories partially overlap, preventing a clear categorization (Cuevas 1994; Hébert and Link 2006). These facts may serve as evidence for what
Low and MacMillan (1988, 140) described as a multifaceted phenomenon. Nevertheless, Cantillon described the entrepreneur first as profit-oriented. Furthermore, three
main traditions can be identified that have characterized the entrepreneur. These include the profit-oriented (modern) Austrian tradition (in accordance with Cantillon)

---

[34] Léon Walras, 1834–1910, was inspired to follow his father into the study of economics. After years of
financial difficulties, Walras lectured at the University of Lausanne in 1870 (Walras 2005, xvff)
[35] Ronald Coase, 1910–2013, was awarded the Nobel Prize in economics in 1991 (Putterman and
Kroszner 1996, 89), and was a as professor at Chicago University where he focused on Chinese capital-
ism (University of Chicago 2013).

and the German and Chicago traditions, which describe the entrepreneur as innovation-oriented.

4.2 Entrepreneurship's Theoretical Categorization

It is clear from the previous subchapter that the term *entrepreneurship* has different meanings to different people. Therefore, several efforts have been made to characterize it. For example, Gartner (1990, 27) used the Delphi method to discover that the majority (79 percent) of participants focused on characteristics of entrepreneurship while the minority focused on the entrepreneurship's outcomes. However, in the end, Gartner concluded that no unambiguous definition can be found (28). Bruyat and Julien (2000, 171) correspondingly argued that *"[d]efining the entrepreneur using attributes [...] generates confusion or leads to tautology"* because, in accordance with Anderson and Starnawska (2008), entrepreneurship is most often used as a noun while the entrepreneur is viewed as a state of being. If someone starts to peel this "intellectual onion," nothing results but tears (Anderson and Starnawska 2008). Hence, Yeung (2009, 210) aptly concluded that *"[...] a precise definition of who (or what) an entrepreneur is"* has not yet been found, and furthermore *the* definition for entrepreneurship may never be found.

How then can entrepreneurship be described if *the* definition does not exist and it is very difficult to derive any definition? Yet, entrepreneurship must be characterized in order to discuss ubiquitous entrepreneurship. As Gartner (1990, 28) stated *"[i]f many different meanings for entrepreneurship exist, then it behooves us to make sure that others know what we are talking about."* Therefore, this book uses Cuevas' all-embracing approach: Instead of creating another definition, Cuevas (1994, 77) provided a characterization *"[...] to construct an ordered and systematized synthesis of the main contributions [...]."*

As Figure 5 indicates, Richard Cantillon is the father of the French tradition, and according to Cuevas (Cuevas 1994, 79), can be seen as the basic precursor to the physio-

crats.[36] According to this school of thought, "*[...] farming with horse-drawn ploughs [...]*
is undertaken by entrepreneurial farmers [...]" where the net-product depends on "*[...]*
the capital intensity of agriculture" (Eltis 1975, 169–171). Subchapter 4.1 highlights
Cantillon's theory. As shown in Figure 5, Cantillon influenced the German-Austrian,
Chicago, and modern Austrian traditions as well the noneconomic tradition, which are
also briefly summarized in subchapter 4.1. In addition, the previous chapter described
the theories of Walras (Walker 1986) and Coase (1937), but omits the theories of the
physiocrats, classics, and Marxists. Cuevas (1994, 85) pointed out that these "*[...] consider the 'capitalist' function as the only or at least most important element in entrepreneurship.*"

According to Cuevas (1994, 86), three entrepreneurial functions can be derived from
the theories listed in Figure 5:

(1) The *Financial Sphere*, which "*[...] corresponds with the traditional 'capitalist'
    function and to a greater extend, with the formal ownership of the firm
    [...][which] incorporates the shareholder or any other type of owner in equity fi-
    nancing.*".

(2) The *Management Sphere*, which allows managerial or directorial agents to su-
    pervise decisions "*[...] and organize the productive process in the distinct areas
    or parcels of the company, but in contrast to the other functional spheres, [...]
    [they do] not assume any entrepreneurial risks.*"

(3) The *'Booster' Sphere*, which contributes to less tangible functions and "*[...] in-
    volve[s] certain risks which accompany any business venture. However, in con-
    trast to the strictly capitalist sphere which is limited to the investment or finan-
    cial resources in a given project, the 'booster' takes on even greater risks [...].*"

---

[36] François Quesnay, who publishes his first article at the age of 62, shaped the physiocratic system. He
stated that agriculture produces a "net product" over certain costs (Eltis 1975, 167)

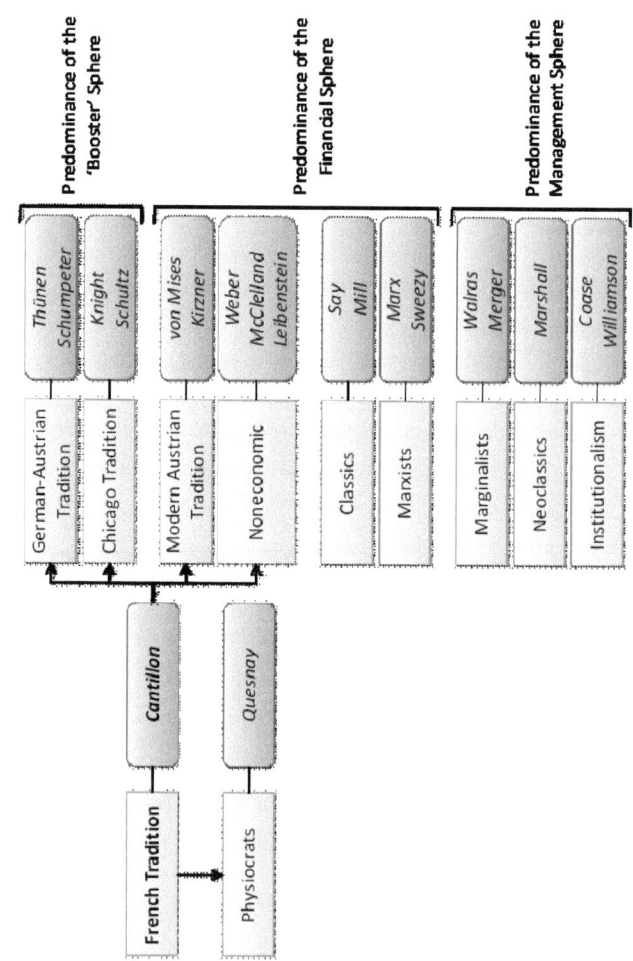

Figure 5: Taxonomy of entrepreneurship. (Source: Own representation based on Cuevas [1994, 84].)

Considering these spheres of entrepreneurship against the background of small firms, the entrepreneur generates joined functions of the financial, management, and "booster" sphere when a small corporation is established. In contrast, in large firms, these functional spheres drift apart (Cuevas 1994, 88). As Figure 6 shows, in small firms the three spheres coexist due to one or several entrepreneurs in one company, whereas in big firms the spheres move apart because the firm must focus separately on these functions and specialization is needed. The three spheres' moving apart in big firms is exactly what Coase (1937, 394) emphasized when he stated that entrepreneurship loses its central function in larger firms. Nevertheless, each sphere is necessary, but the overlap is smaller because of specialization.

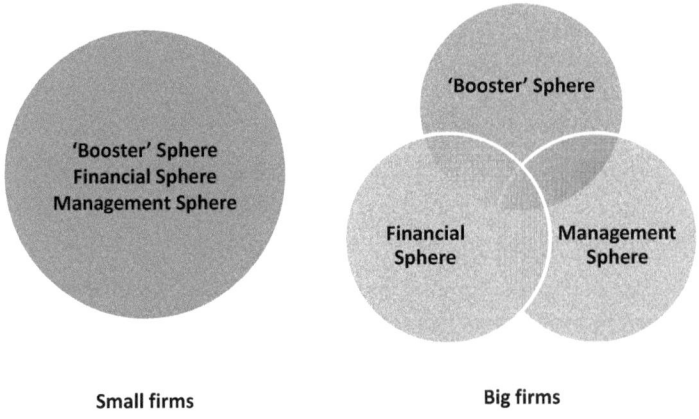

Small firms   **Big firms**

Figure 6: Components of entrepreneurship. (Source: Own representation based on Cuevas [1994, 85].)

To summarize, Cuevas' (1994) approach does not deliver a precise definition of entrepreneurship, and this definition does not exist. Instead, he presented a holistic approach derived out of the history of entrepreneurship's theories. A discussion of ubiquitous entrepreneurship (Chapter 5) benefits from Cuevas' (1994) characterization because his approach includes several theories and outlines three spheres that characterize and promote entrepreneurship. These spheres are the risk-oriented "booster" sphere, the profit-oriented financial sphere, and the supervision-oriented management sphere.

4.3 Importance of Entrepreneurship

According to Wennekers and Thurik (1999, 51), entrepreneurship matters! Wadhwa et al. (2009, 4) even stated that *"[e]ntrepreneurs are among the most celebrated people in our culture."* This subchapter provides a short overview of why entrepreneurship is important for modern societies and why it should be promoted. However, a detailed description of these concepts is beyond the scope of this book, and the literature cited here is highly recommended for further study. Subchapter 4.3.1 describes how entrepreneurship contributes to economy. Next, the problem of social exclusion is briefly addressed in subchapter 4.3.2), and finally, European entrepreneurship projects are introduced in 4.3.3.

4.3.1 Entrepreneurship and Economy

Iyigun and Owen (1998, 454) stated that *"[e]ntrepreneurs provide the economy with new ideas, products, and ways of doing things [...],"* which are activities that are basic for a healthy economy. Wennekers and Thurik (1999, 34) agreed, stating that entrepreneurship is linked to economic growth through startups, innovations, and competition. After a detailed analysis, they concluded that entrepreneurship is more important than ever because of globalization and the predominance of IT (51). Finally, Wennekers and Thurik highlighted that entrepreneurship is linked to economic growth on three levels: On the individual level, the entrepreneur has certain attitudes and skills, which on the second level are prerequisites for innovative startups, and then lead to a competitive selection in which economic growth is created (1999, 51). Additionally, Audretsch (2007) emphasized that entrepreneurship generates economic growth. But instead of focusing on various fields of literature like Wennekers and Thurik, Audretsch viewed entrepreneurship as the *"[...] missing link between investments in new knowledge and economic growth"* (65). Uncommercialized knowledge created in an organizational context, Audretsch argued, is the source for new entrepreneurial opportunities, which can be used to facilitate knowledge spillovers, and in turn, can contribute to economic growth (69). (See subchapter 4.1 for how the view on entrepreneurship has changed over the years.) While Schultz (1980, 438), as a founder of the Chicago tradition, argued that the entrepreneur's contribution to economic growth is concealed in national income accounting, Wennekers and Thurik as well as Audretsch explicitly pointed out that entrepreneurship directly contributes to economic growth.

4.3.2 Social Inclusion and Migrant Entrepreneurship

The European Union (EU) also recognizes and promotes the contribution of entrepreneurship to economic growth. With the Lisbon strategy,[37] the EU began to facilitate entrepreneurship (Atkinson et al. 2004, 49) to combat social exclusion, among other things. Bolt et al. (1998, 85) supported position when they stated that social homogeneity can generate *"[...] an economic base for all kinds of entrepreneurship"* if immigrants have certain entrepreneurial capacities (89). As the Organization for Economic Co-operation and Development (OECD) pointed out, these capacities are based on culture, access to capital, or success rates (OECD 2010). Finally, the OECD advised that entrepreneurship among migrants should be supported to increase the prospects of their success (2010, 25).

But social exclusion does not refer only to migrants. According to Fielden and Dawe (2004), women entrepreneurs should be supported, too. In their research, they found that women in the United Kingdom, especially those with lower socioeconomic backgrounds, did not see themselves as potential entrepreneurs (2004, 140). Fielden and Dawe concluded that women entrepreneurs have great potential and that *"[...] the vast pool of entrepreneurial talent [...] is waiting to be unlocked"* (141).

4.3.3 Entrepreneurship Projects

The EU has begun several projects to release entrepreneurial potential among various social classes. From 2007 to 2013, for example, the European Commission (2013a)

---

[37] The EU's Lisbon strategy was launched in 2000 to foster the EU's emergence as a competitive knowledge-based economy with sustainable economic growth through 2010 by unlocking business potential through the promotion of entrepreneurship, among other things (European Commission 2010a). Nowadays, the Europe 2020 strategy, successor to the Lisbon strategy, puts forward priorities in economic growth based on knowledge as well as innovation, making full use of IT in combination with entrepreneurship (European Commission 2010b).

launched the Competitiveness and Innovation Framework Program[38] (CIP). One of CIP's three parts is the Entrepreneurship and Innovation Program (EIP) to foster the entrepreneurship culture in the EU (European Commission 2013b). Finally, the EIP has led to the EU's so called Entrepreneurship Action Plan 2020, a blueprint to unleash entrepreneurial potential in Europe (European Commission 2013d). With this action plan the EU promotes further entrepreneurship education and more innovation, with the believe that entrepreneurship will have positive effects on economic growth and entrepreneurship education will positively influence young people's mindsets (European Commission 2012, 7). Hence, the EU's key message is to improve entrepreneurship education within higher education, and make entrepreneurship education obligatory throughout all disciplines (European Commission 2012, 82–86).

But the extension into all disciplines refers not only to higher education; the European Commission also promotes women's entrepreneurship, migrants' entrepreneurship, and several other projects, with information that can be found on the Internet (European Commission 2013e).

Finally, another national initiative that should be highlighted is EXIST[39] program, which the German and the European Social Fund cofinanced. The goal of EXIST is to move from innovation to enterprise and from researcher to entrepreneur (Federal Ministry of Economics and Technology [BMWi] 2013a). Thus, the support program has three parts: first, to support the entrepreneurial culture in universities; second, to support startups through entrepreneurial scholarship; and third, to increase startups' feasibility through research transfer (Federal Ministry of Economics and Technology [BMWi] 2013a). Currently, EXIST is in its fourth phase, in which universities are improving their startup management to position themselves as entrepreneurial university (Federal Ministry of Economics and Technology [BMWi] 2013b). Further information regarding

---

[38] The successor to the CIP is called Program for the Competitiveness of Enterprises and SMEs (COSME) and will operate from 2014 to 2020. COSME continues the CIP's goals, and entrepreneurs are expected to be able to access financing more easily, which may increase their ranks (European Commission 2013c).
[39] A German promotion program, EXIST is an acronym for *Existenzgründungen aus der Wissenschaft*(Federal Ministry of Economics and Technology [BMWi] 2013a). The first phase of the EXIST project began in 1998, followed by three more phases in 2002, 2006, and 2010 (Federal Ministry of Economics and Technology [BMWi] 2013b).

the EXIST program in Germany can be found in *Scientific Entrepreneurship: Reflections on Success of 10 Years EXIST* (Von Kortzfleisch 2011).

5 Ubiquitous Entrepreneurship

Based on previous research, this chapter presents how scientific entrepreneurship can become ubiquitous. Subchapter 5.1 begins with a glance back into history to show how the university's mission has changed over the years. Two academic revolutions are described, the latter of which promotes an entrepreneurial university to actively develop economics and society in this time. Finally, subchapter 5.1 distinguishes between academic entrepreneurship, representing the institutional view, and scientific entrepreneurship, representing the functional view. Subchapter 5.2 focuses on scientific entrepreneurship engineering, a modern and holistic view of scientific entrepreneurship using the engineering paradigm to achieve objectives for certain action fields with the methods and operationally applied instruments. Subchapter 5.2 also emphasizes the methods and instruments that can be used to support the three entrepreneurial spheres — the booster, the financial, and the management (see subchapter 4.2) — which means that they support entrepreneurship in its entirety. Subchapter 5.3 goes one step further and shows how the characteristics describing ubiquity in humanities (subchapter 2.3) and in information technology (subchapter 3.2) can be used to derive a framework to promote ubiquitous scientific entrepreneurship. For a better understanding, a ubiquitous entrepreneurship board is developed and introduced.

5.1 Scientific Entrepreneurship

Chapter 4 highlighted how entrepreneurship can be characterized, how it contributes to the economy, and how entrepreneurship has been promoted through several initiatives in higher education. For example, the European Commission clearly requires the promotion of an entrepreneurial culture beginning with school education (European Commission 2013e). Besides the current projects, Theodore Schultz (1980, 448) as one founder of the Chicago tradition (see subchapter 4.1) claimed that education can enhance entrepreneurship. In addition, Wadhwa et al. (2009, 9) showed that the vast majority of entrepreneurs are well educated, with approximately 95 percent holding bachelor's degrees (48 percent) or higher (47 percent).[40] Furthermore, they pointed out that approximately 41 percent of students who are "extremely interested" in starting a business during their university years take five years or less to start their own companies (2009, 16). Therefore, ubiquitous scientific entrepreneurship focuses on a broad group of potential entrepreneurs in academia and has the potential to reduce the time taken to start a business by increasing interest in entrepreneurship. Hence, this chapter ties in with entrepreneurship in higher education and focuses on scientific entrepreneurship with the entrepreneurial university at its center.

For a better understanding of how entrepreneurship is linked to higher education, this chapter starts with a history of the entrepreneurial university. According to Oliveira (2000, 24), the development towards the entrepreneurial university began at the end of the Middle Ages. During that time, the university was not independent, but was used to defend God, the emperor, and country (Bertilsson 1992, 334). The university's main function in the Middle Ages was teaching the predominant doctrine. However, with the secularization of the 17th century, the university edged away from the church (Fuller 1997, 484). Gorski (2000, 139) stated that a single secularization process did not exist, but that several theories dealt with secularization, which had in common a *differentiation thesis*, meaning that religious and nonreligious institutions differentiate over time. Hence, the university has shifted its dependence from the church to the to the state (Oliveira 2000, 24). In addition, Tschannen (1991, 398) added that rationalization could be viewed as the main carrier of the secularization process and as a reason for the dependency shift.

The next step towards the entrepreneurial university in Germany occurred at the end of the 18th century when the so-called *research university* was developed. In Germany with its predominant particularism, small states compete against each other but are open-minded to universities (Bertilsson 1992, 335). In 1810, Berlin University, also known as the Humboldtian[41] university, was organized *"[...] around its own research*

---

[40] For this research, the Global Engineering and Entrepreneurship project at Duke University surveyed 549 entrepreneurs from various industries (Wadhwa et al. 2009, 4).
[41] Alexander von Humboldt (1769–1859) was a German scientist and researcher. In 1810, Humboldt was in charge of the Prussian education system, and over 14 months, convinced Prussian King Friedrich Wil-

and teaching [...] [and] expresses[ed] a complex of knowledge independent of church and state. The university should be a 'republic' within the state – with its own 'senate,' own 'citizens,' and guardians" (Bertilsson 1992, 335) so that in the end, the university is comparatively independent from state, economy, and society (Oliveira 2000, 25). This independent university creates a new, independent type of knowledge, as opposed to religious knowledge. As Oliveira (2000, 24) indicated, this approach can be described as science, in that in addition to teaching, the university also creates scientific knowledge as its second mission. Furthermore, innovative methodological techniques like seminars, arising out of philological research or teaching laboratories and invented at the German Giessen University, helped students to gain a better understanding of science (Etzkowitz 2002, 10). The development from a teaching and knowledge conservation institution to a research university in which science emerges is known as the *first academic revolution* (Etzkowitz 2003, 317) and shaped the modern university (Robins & Webster 2002, 34). Although, the first academic revolution added research to teaching (Etzkowitz 1998, 823), one additional step is needed to move from a research university to an entrepreneurial university (Etzkowitz 2003, 317).

The idea of a research university spread from Germany to other countries, including the United States. Thus, German doctoral mentors often inspire professors at teaching institutions like Harvard to initiate research programs (Etzkowitz 2002, 11). However, until the late 19th century, US universities made no clear distinction between mostly theory-based basic research and applied research (Etzkowitz 2002, 11). During this time, the Massachusetts Institute of Technology (MIT), founded in 1862, displaced Harvard as a model because of MIT's combination of basic research and teaching with industrial innovation (Etzkowitz 2002, 12). Furthermore, World War II changed the separation between basic and applied research because scientists from a basic research culture were enlisted to work in war-related engineering projects, closing the gap between pure science and engineering (Etzkowitz 2002, 12). Therefore, in the

---

helm III to reject the French university model (state-controlled higher education reserved for higher civil servants or officers) in favor of a modern university in Berlin, independent of church and state (Rüegg 2011, 11, 598).

mid-20th century, a *second academic revolution* occurred, advancing the entrepre-neurial university (Etzkowitz 2002, 40) with the transfer of research into new enter-prises and products (Etzkowitz et al. 1998, 1). Hence, as the first academic revolution spread to science, the second was set in motion and is ongoing (Etzkowitz 2002, 12, 40).

In 1945, an entrepreneurship course was introduced at Harvard Business School ap-parently to attract students returning from military service and to respond to the col-lapsing weapons industries (Vesper and Gartner 1997, 406). A year after World War II, a venture capital firm called the American Research and Development Corporation (ARD) combined MIT's technical expertise with Harvard's business expertise to provide business advice and tutorials on starting a firm to potential entrepreneurs in the aca-demic world (Etzkowitz 2002, 4). This newly developed academic model created a new mission for the university: to build up a venture capital industry in the early post-war period (Etzkowitz 2002, 4). Finally, this new model of an entrepreneurial university integrated economic development as a third academic mission in addition to teaching and research (Etzkowitz 1998, 833). Etzkowitz (1998, 833) called this the *capitalization of knowledge "[...] linking universities to users of knowledge more tightly and establish-ing the [entrepreneurial] university as an economic actor in its own right."* Table 4 briefly summarizes the expansion of the mission of the university, beginning with teaching in the Middle Ages, followed by research after the first academic revolution, and finally entrepreneurship aimed at developing the economies and society.[42]

Table 4: Expansion of the university's mission.(Source: Own representation based on Etzkowitz [2003, 110].)

Teaching	Research	Entrepreneurship
Knowledge reservation and dissemination	*First academic revolution*	*Second academic revolution*

---

[42] Additionally, Viale and Etzkowitz (2005, 2) described a third academic revolution that focused on social transformation, stating the *"the entrepreneurial university becomes the center of gravity for economic development, knowledge creation, and diffusion in both advanced industrial and developing societies."*

Teaching	Research	Entrepreneurship
First mission:	Second mission:	Third mission:
teaching;	research;	economic and social
new missions generate	first mission continues	development through en-
conflict of interest		trepreneurship;
controversies		old missions continue

In the following years, the entrepreneurship course at Harvard grew in popularity even though entrepreneurship, as Vesper and Gartner (1997, 406) described it, was not fashionable then. Nevertheless, in the 1950s and 1960s, high-tech firms began to locate closer to universities, such as Hewlett-Packard's locating in the Stanford Industrial Park[43] (Etzkowitz 2002, 4), an indication that academic technology transfer into industry was becoming more important. In the 1970s, entrepreneurship became a chief focus of mainstream business presses, filling books and articles (Finkle and Deeds 2001, 616), or as Etzkowitz and Leydesdorff (2000, 110) stated, it led to a reevaluation of the university's mission and role in society.

According to Henrekson (2005, 440), several other reasons can be found for the popularity of the entrepreneurial university: In the 1970s, the predominance of large firms was challenged as smaller firms were being founded in the service industry, which is based on an entrepreneurial character and therefore, more related to innovation and growth. Furthermore, consumers' demands for more differentiated products led to an increase in small entrepreneurial firms (Henrekson 2005, 440). As a result, the entrepreneurial university played a central role in contributing to economic growth. Universities became important for knowledge production as well as the identification of future trends impacting society (Etzkowitz et al. 2000, 326). Along with entrepreneurship's great success, entrepreneurship courses in business schools increased in the 1970s (Vesper and Gartner 1997, 406).

---

[43] In 1951, the Stanford Industrial Park was founded for light industry, providing an additional source of income for the financially struggling university. The idea behind this park was to build close relationships between Stanford and industry. Its huge success necessitated an expansion of the park in 1960 to more than double its originally size. As the companies spread out towards San Francisco in the north and San Jose in the south, the region was called Silicon Valley, first mentioned in an *Electronics News* article from 1971 (Sandelin, 2004).

The 1980s were marked by a greater technology transfer from university to industry, which can be traced back to *"[t]he US Bayh-Dole Act of 1980 and its European counterparts [...] [which encouraged] universities to patent inventions funded by federal agencies"* (Rothaermel et al. 2007, 695). The act ensured that intellectual property from federally funded research could be used to receive government funds (Etzkowitz 2002, 4). As the demand for technological innovation continued, entrepreneurship courses at universities increased as well (Rothaermel et al. 2007, 695). According to Vesper and Gartner (1997, 406), several universities began to offer more than one course in entrepreneurship, clustering these courses into entrepreneurship programs.

The number of research articles relating to entrepreneurship is another measure of its increasing importance. For example, Rothaermel et al. (2007, 696) noted that the number of published articles since 1996 increased to more than five per year, reaching a peak in 2005 with 20 published research articles.[44] Clearly, researchers at universities had become recognized as key sources for innovation as they published their results and informed others of their innovations (Von Hippel 1988, 18).

Along with this positive trend, German governmental institutions began to initiate publicly funded programs – such as the EXIS program discussed in subchapter 4.3.3 – as the importance of entrepreneurship for German universities was recognized (Von Kortzfleisch 2011, 3). Begun in 1998 in five model regions, EXIST now promotes startups throughout Germany (Federal Ministry of Economics and Technology [BMWi] 2013b). According to the positive trend that Rothaermel et al. (2007) identified, reasonable endeavors are being made to promote entrepreneurship at German universities. Entrepreneurship has different meanings (see subchapters 4.1 and 4.2), and universities have to distinguish between academic and scientific entrepreneurship.

Several researchers use academic entrepreneurship as a synonym for knowledge commercialization. For example, Henrekson and Rosenberg (2000, 1) viewed academic entrepreneurship similar to that described earlier in this chapter: a development process after World War II in which universities created potentially useful knowledge to

---

[44] Rothaermel et al. (2007) analyze the published research articles over a period of 24 years ending in 2005 (cf. Rothaermel, et al., 2007, p. 696).

contribute to economic growth in various ways. Braunerhjelm (2007, 620) also described academic entrepreneurship similarly, stating that academic entrepreneurship is one of several channels that can be used to apply knowledge into goods and services. In addition, Etzkowitz (2003, 119) described academic entrepreneurship as both endogenous and exogenous: *"It is endogenous in the sense that it is an internal development within academia that emanates from the way that the research university grew up. On the other hand, university-based innovation is in part the result of external influences […]."*

A differentiation between academic and scientific entrepreneurship is necessary at this point before the characteristics for ubiquity can be applied to the latter. According to Sijde et al. (2002), Grichnik et al. (2009) and von Kortzfleisch (2011, 4) emphasized that academic entrepreneurship represents the *institutional view* of entrepreneurial universities, in which specific, supportive, and institutional settings are developed to stimulate entrepreneurship in academia. Furthermore, von Kortzfleisch (2011, 4) pointed out that researchers have focused mainly on the institutional view and have investigated the entrepreneurial university against a specific institutional scope, omitting the *functional view.* According to Grichnik et al. (2009, 172), scientific entrepreneurship focuses on the less frequently investigated functional view, in which appropriate methods and instruments are used to create startups from business ideas stemming from academic research. In that context, "Sylter Runde," a German group of researchers who analyzed economics, science, and culture, initially described scientific entrepreneurship (Sylter Runde 2013). They stated that the scientific entrepreneur is *"an entrepreneurial-oriented promoter in the academic community, who creates and modernizes institutional structures through invention, innovation, and transformation by using specific methods and instruments"* (Von Kortzfleisch 2011, 4).[45] This definition

---

[45] Von Kortzfleisch (2011) translated the German definition for a scientific entrepreneur into English (von Kortzfleisch 2011, 4), and his translation is used in this thesis. The original German definition can be found in the memorandum of the 18th Sylter Runde (2007): *"Ein Scientific Entrepreneur ist ein unternehmerisch ausgerichteter Promotor im wissenschaftlichen Umfeld, der unter Verwendung gründungsorientierter Methoden und Instrumente über Invention, Innovation und Transformation gezielt entsprechende institutionelle Strukturen schafft bzw. vorhandene nutzt oder unter effektiven und effizienten Aspekten modernisiert."*

emphasizes the key role of a scientific entrepreneur as a promoter, who is able to rapidly implement innovative ideas with the help of certain methods and instruments.

In conclusion, the mission of the university has expanded, from teaching, into research, and finally to the focus on entrepreneurship. The entrepreneurial university plays a major role for entrepreneurship in academia, which can be classified into academic entrepreneurship as the institutional view and scientific entrepreneurship as the functional view.

5.2 Scientific Entrepreneurship Engineering

This subchapter links the engineering paradigm to scientific engineering according to Magin and von Kortzfleisch (2008). Therefore, four one-dimensional approaches are briefly introduced that form the basis for Magin and von Kortzfleisch's (2008) holistic view.

According to the engineering paradigm, methods and instruments are usually used to carry out complex tasks in engineering disciplines (Von Kortzfleisch 2011, 4); however, scientific entrepreneurship obviously is not an engineering discipline. Nevertheless, the engineering paradigm is commonly applied to nonengineering sciences like in computer science in which software development process is professionalized to meet steadily increasing requirements, or in economic science, especially the service development process, in which rapidly growing product-service bundles, market convergences, or competition requires process professionalization (Von Kortzfleisch 2011, 4). Magin and von Kortzfleisch (2008, 4) were the first to adopt a holistic, systematic, and sustainable engineering approach that transferred these methods and instruments to entrepreneurship. To create a holistic approach, Magin and von Kortzfleisch (2008) first aggregated the various theoretical scientific entrepreneurship initiatives, each of which emphasized only a portion of scientific entrepreneurship, into four approaches: *"The aim of this categorization is not to evaluate and compare the different approaches to one another, but to make these different perspectives transparent and to learn from them in order to address scientific entrepreneurship more effectively"* (Von Kortzfleisch 2011, 6). Until 2008, the approaches available were these four:

(1) The *task-role matching approach*, which originated with the European Forum for Entrepreneurship Research (EFER), matches entrepreneurial tasks with specific entrepreneurial roles represented by stakeholders of scientific entrepreneurship (EFER 2006). Therefore, the university plays a key role in considering the various instruments when promoting scientific entrepreneurship. Even though these instruments are not chronologically or hierarchically they can be seen as equivalent and interacting. However, this approach vastly simplifies startup promotion in academia due to missing methods and the lack of specified stakeholder cross-linking (Magin and von Kortzfleisch 2008, 10).

(2) According to the EU's Lisbon strategy (see subchapter 4.3.2), the *deficit-oriented approach* promotes scientific entrepreneurship by identifying deficits in scientific entrepreneurship initiatives based on empirical data, and then improving those initiatives to promote quick-start, fast-growing initiatives (Twaalfhoven 2004, 1). This approach evaluates scientific entrepreneurship on aggregated levels, but neither describes how concrete instruments can be implemented nor recommends concrete actions to reach an ideal state (Magin and von Kortzfleisch 2008, 11–13).

(3) The *process-oriented approach*, such as Ashmore's (2005, 7) entrepreneurship education process, is a phase-based approach that defines objectives and instruments within each phase. This time-dependent view is often used to describe entrepreneurial processes with varying granularity. Although this approach considers certain instruments in a time-dependent manner, target groups are addressed imprecisely (Magin and von Kortzfleisch 2008, 14)

(4) The *resource-based approach* is a management-based view on enterprises that can be transferred to entrepreneurship, according to Magin and von Kortzfleisch (2008, 16). This approach goes back to Penrose (1959, 75), who emphasized the heterogeneous nature of entrepreneurial services. For scientific entrepreneurship, this approach implies that entrepreneurs have access to certain resources, namely material infrastructure, finance, human resources, social networks, resource organizations, and technical resources (Magin and von Kortzfleisch 2008, 16–18). Even though this approach is based on already

sensitized entrepreneurial target-groups, it is not clear how instruments have to be used (18).

Magin and von Kortzfleisch (2008, 18) criticized these four approaches for their one-dimensional views, their indifference in implementing instruments, and their lack of sustainable evaluation. Therefore, with the help of the engineering paradigm, they sought to integrate the approaches into a holistic framework. As shown in Figure 7, this framework includes 13 action fields, which are briefly summarized according to Grichnik et al. (2009) and von Kortzfleisch (2011).

Students and researchers must be *sensitized* to increase the motivation of startup creation out of academia. The *entrepreneurial culture* is directly connected to sensitization in order to promote scientific entrepreneurship because a culture that makes entrepreneurship visible in academia also sensitizes students and researchers. As seen in Figure 7, both action fields – sensitization and entrepreneurial culture – lead to a quantitative growth of startups. Therefore, potential ideas must be *identified* systematically to promote the entrepreneurial process at an early stage. Afterwards, students and researchers must promote innovative *ideas* so that their creativity can generate innovation and their scientific work is published and spurs further research. In addition, *teams* are the formula for success because strong multidisciplinary groups create a common entrepreneurial culture in which ideas can be brought forward. This stable relationship can also be promoted by *social networks*, which facilitate interactions within the community and ease *mentoring*, a necessity for successful startup creation. Moreover, entrepreneurial competencies must be promoted by providing entrepreneurial *knowledge* in the best possible way, such as with learning platforms.

Figure 7 shows that *financial resources* as well as *material infrastructures* are important for scientific entrepreneurship. Therefore, scientific entrepreneurs be supported financially, for example, through matching investors with the help of social networks. Besides, material infrastructure – especially information and communications infrastructure or access to rooms – helps promote innovative startups, particularly considering the necessary spatial proximity between rooms and universities. However, to ensure continuous development of any action fields, *evaluation* procedures must be implemented (Von Kortzfleisch 2011, 10); therefore, *motivation* must be used to overcome uncertainty and increase commitment to the success of scientific entrepreneurship (Grichnik et al. 2009, 182; von Kortzfleisch 2011, 8).

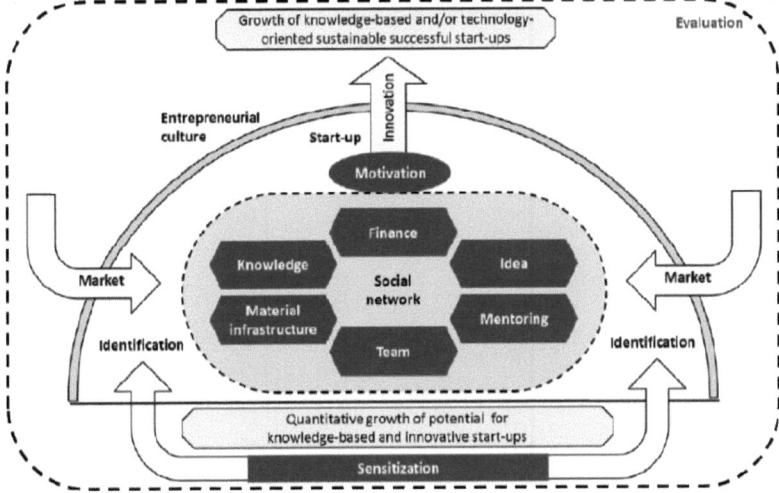

Figure 7: Integrative approach to scientific engineering. (Source: Von Kortzfleisch [2011, 9].)

This holistic and integrated framework from Magin and von Kortzfleisch (2008) meets the engineering paradigm in a way that methods are used to reach the objectives for each action field. Additionally, they also use instruments as operationally applied tools to support those methods (24). For a better understanding of the methods and instruments to use, Table 5 summarizes Magin and von Kortzfleisch's results:[46]

---

[46] Detailed explanations can be found in the German book *Methoden und Instrumente des Scientific Entrepreneurship Engineering* (cf. Magin & von Kortzfleisch, 2008, p. 22ff.).

Table 5: Methods and instruments for scientific entrepreneurship.
(Source: Own representation based on Magin and von Kortzfleisch [2008, 128].)

Action field	Methods	Instruments
Knowledge	Theoretical knowledge Laboratory knowledge Practical knowledge	Lectures and seminars Workshops and simulations Intrapreneurship Internship
Entrepreneurial culture	Values Norms Artifacts	Virtual entrepreneurship net Entrepreneurship days Common infrastructure
Team	Self-assessment Team-building	Questionnaires Workshops Mentor-oriented consulting Competence portfolio
Material infrastructure	Physical proximity between entrepreneurs and university	Access to rooms Research laboratories Information and communication infrastructure
Social network	Face-to-face contacts Virtual networks	Virtual entrepreneurship communities Entrepreneurship days
Finance	Direct support Indirect promotion through matching	Scholarships University as partner matching investors
Motivation	Increasing extrinsic motivation	Acknowledgement of entrepreneurial activities Supporting tutorials
Idea	Creativity techniques Computer-supported idea management	Virtual idea platform Creativity workshops
Mentoring	Combination of mentoring and external consulting	Mentor-oriented consulting

Action field	Methods	Instruments
Sensitization	Direct sensitization	Multiplayer business game
	Multiplier effect	Entrepreneurship lounge

Based on the characteristics identified in subchapter 4.2, the action fields – and their methods and instruments – can be assigned to the three entrepreneurial spheres. As shown in Figure 8, some action fields focus primarily on certain spheres. For example, finance obviously is an action field that is primarily assigned to the financial sphere. Material infrastructure, social network, and mentoring are first and foremost assigned to the management sphere because the main objectives of those fields are to create necessary tangible and intangible infrastructures (Grichnik et al. 2009, 183). As for the action field "idea," a startup must have an idea that is both successful and marketable (Grichnik et al. 2009, 183), and therefore, this action field can be assigned to the booster and the financial spheres. The other action fields – entrepreneurial culture, motivation, sensitization, team, and knowledge – are related to all spheres. For example, the entrepreneurial culture is built on each of the three spheres because students and researchers have to be sensitized and motivated for entrepreneurship as a whole. Finally, the entrepreneurial team should have knowledge in all three spheres to successfully create innovative startups.

Therefore, almost all methods and instruments are relevant when it comes to promoting entrepreneurship within academia. Furthermore, Figure 8 highlights only the primary focus of each action field. For example, the action field social network also may be important for the booster sphere in terms of promoting innovation, and mentoring may influence the financial sphere as it may save costs. Hence, the entrepreneurial university's main objective is to promote all three entrepreneurial spheres using certain methods and instruments to strengthen the scientific entrepreneur as a promoter. The Sylter Runde (2007) defines a scientific entrepreneur as person who takes a key role in the academic community and uses certain methods and instruments.

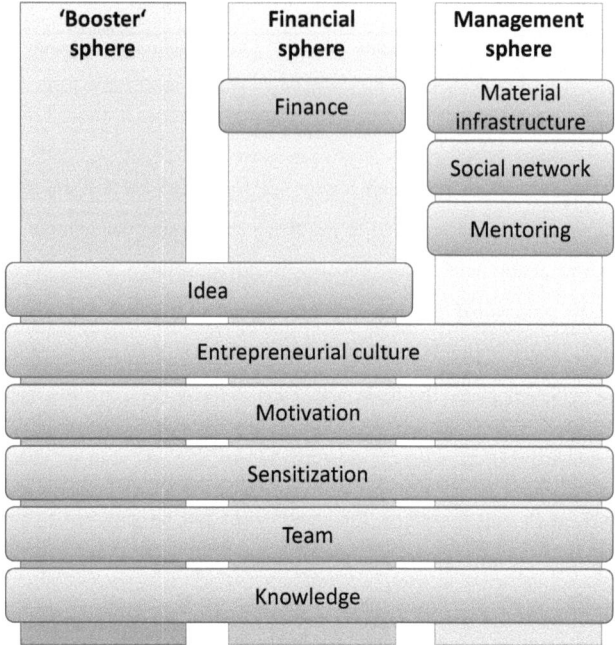

Figure 8: Scientific entrepreneurship's action fields per entrepreneurial sphere. (Source: Own representation.)

To conclude, scientific entrepreneurship's action fields and their corresponding methods and instruments can educate the entrepreneur by promoting the booster, financial, and management spheres to increase startup creation. The key to ubiquity in scientific entrepreneurship is the widespread use of certain methods and instruments to educate potential entrepreneurs. First, the majority of the methods and instruments support all three entrepreneurial spheres, which increases the personal skills mandatory for successful entrepreneurship. Second, Magin and von Kortzfleisch (2008) showed that these methods and instruments are key tools to successful startup creation because they increase the knowledge-based outcome of scientific entrepreneurship. Hence, the more ubiquitous the methods and instruments in the entrepreneurial university, the more ubiquitous scientific entrepreneurship will be on both the personal and the outcome level.

5.3 Impacts from Humanities and Information Technology on the Ubiquity of Scientific Entrepreneurship

To make scientific entrepreneurship ubiquitous, the characteristics of ubiquity in the humanities and in IT, described in Chapter 2 and Chapter 3, are applied to scientific entrepreneurship. Hence, this subchapter takes a similar approach as Magin and von Kortzfleisch (2008), who transferred the engineering paradigm to scientific entrepreneurship (subchapter 5.2). This section compares the characteristics of ubiquity and then uses them as determinants to develop a framework to transfer these traits to scientific entrepreneurship. The basis of this framework comprises the five W-questions, which describe context awareness, according to Table 2. Therefore, context awareness is the key determinant within this framework. Each of the five Ws is answered to include one or more characteristics for ubiquity, and how the methods and instruments can used to finally reach ubiquity in scientific entrepreneurship is demonstrated. Finally, the ubiquitous entrepreneurship board is used to summarize the characteristics regarding each W-question.

5.3.1 Framework Development

In the previous chapters, 14 sources were identified as describing ubiquity in either theology or IT. The identified characteristics from theology and from IT are shown in Figure 9.

Characteristics for Ubiquity per Religion

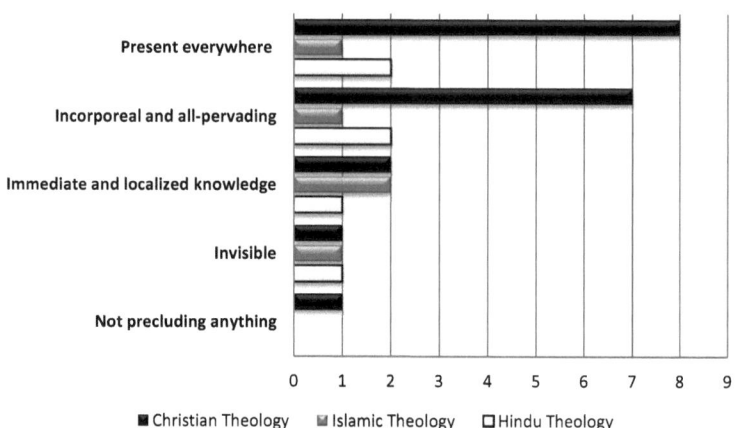

■ Christian Theology   ▨ Islamic Theology   ☐ Hindu Theology

Characteristics for Ubiquity in IT

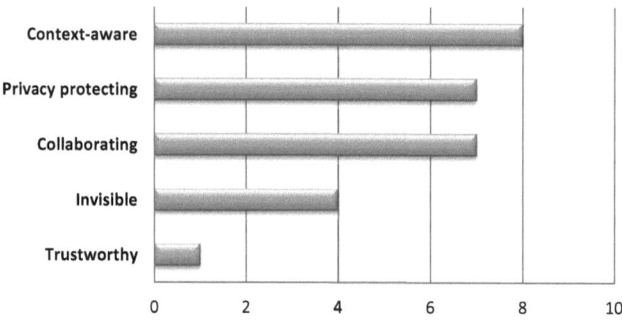

Figure 9: Comparison of characteristics for ubiquity from theology and IT. (Source: Own representation.)

Furthermore, ubiquity is attributed as being invisible in theology as well as in IT. However, invisibility seems to be slightly more important in IT than in religion. Being trustworthy and not precluding anything play a subordinated role because each characteristic is identified only once. Nevertheless, both should be considered for reaching ubiquity in entrepreneurship.

As mentioned, the characteristics from theology and IT serve as determinants for a framework for examining how scientific entrepreneurship can be ubiquitous. Therefore, the identified characteristics must be transferred into this framework utilizing context awareness: First, context awareness is most frequently mentioned in IT to reach ubiquity, and, second, IT's characteristics are more specific, and context awareness is described with the five W-questions, according to Table 2. Thus, if context-awareness is the basis of this framework, it mainly includes the questions What?, Where?, Who?, When?, and Why? For ubiquitous entrepreneurship, the answers to these questions should include the identified characteristics so that ubiquity can be reached within scientific entrepreneurship. Furthermore, transferring these characteristics to scientific entrepreneurship also means that the entrepreneurial university and the three entrepreneurial spheres are taken into consideration as well as the methods and instruments that promote the three spheres. The entrepreneurial university is a requirement for ubiquitous scientific entrepreneurship focusing on the booster, financial, and management sphere with methods and tools promoting them. With the determinants from theology and IT, these methods and instruments are used to reach ubiquity.

To summarize, the framework consists of two parts: The first is the general framework as shown in Figure 10. The entrepreneurial university with its booster, financial, and management spheres uses certain methods and instruments to promote scientific entrepreneurship (Magin and von Kortzfleisch 2008). However, these methods and instruments can be enhanced as required, which is why they are labeled with a plus sign. Context awareness, expressed by the five W questions serves as the basis to reach ubiquity.

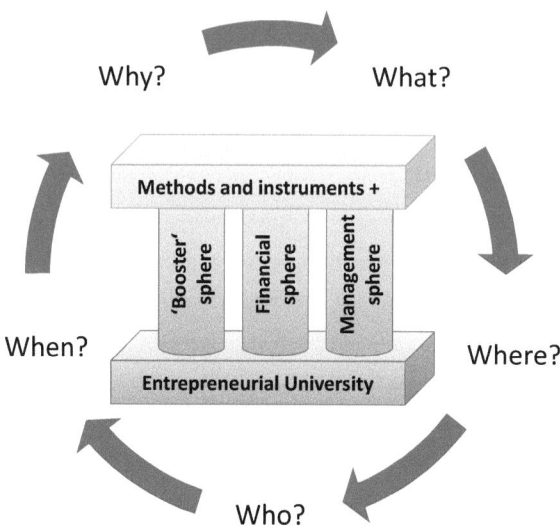

Figure 10: General framework for ubiquitous entrepreneurship. (Source: Own representation.)

Second, the "Ubiquitous Entrepreneurship Board" is depicted in Table 6, which is used to assign the characteristics for ubiquity to each of the five W questions, to meet the requirement of context awareness. The characteristics for ubiquity serve as general requirements for each question, and each determinant can be assigned to a specific question. Finally, the board includes an individual section because each university must define for itself what it means to be an entrepreneurial university based on the three spheres. Furthermore, if the entrepreneurial university is positioned, the methods and instruments can be defined to support the three entrepreneurial spheres. At this point, the individual section must take the general requirements into account so that ubiquity can be reached.

Table 6: Ubiquitous Entrepreneurship Board. (Source: Own representation.)

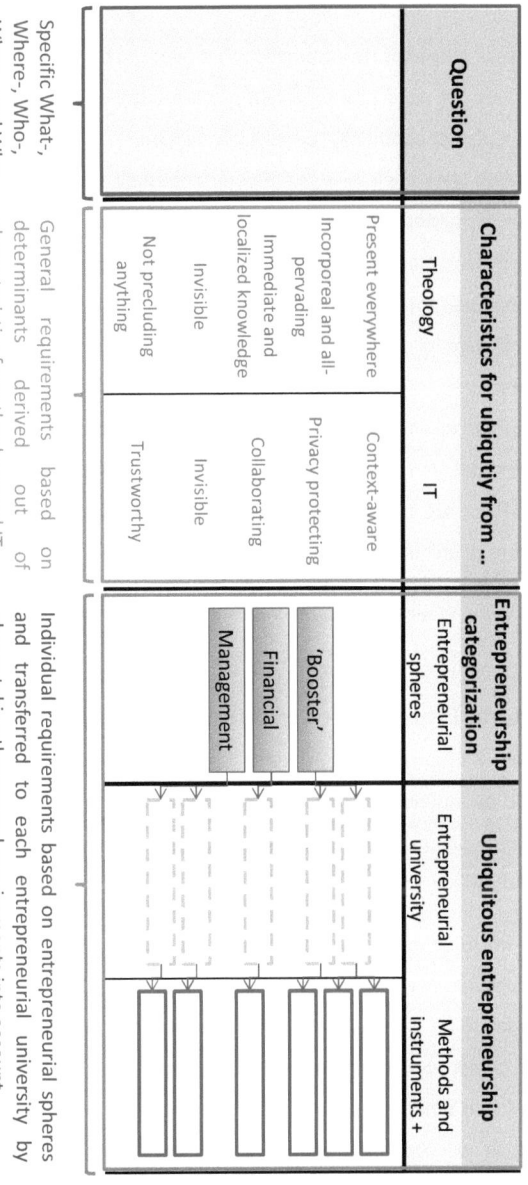

Question	Characteristics for ubiqutiy from ...		Entrepreneurship categorization	Ubiquitous entrepreneurship	
	Theology	IT	Entrepreneurial spheres	Entrepreneurial university	Methods and instruments +
	Present everywhere	Context-aware	Management		
	Incorporeal and all-pervading	Privacy protecting	Financial		
	Immediate and localized knowledge	Collaborating	'Booster'		
	Invisible	Invisible			
	Not precluding anything	Trustworthy			
Specific What-, Where-, Who-, When-, and Why- questions	General requirements based on determinants derived out of characteristics from theology and IT		Individual requirements based on entrepreneurial spheres and transferred to each entrepreneurial university by always taking the general requirements into account		

As data is entered into the ubiquitous entrepreneurship board in the subchapter 5.3.2, the following format is used to express various influences:

(1) Entries in grey indicate information that needs to be taken into account overall, but does not need to be relevant to each question. Hence, these entries will form a pool of potentially relevant information.

(2) Entries in black are less relevant to each question. For example, context aware- ness is formatted this way because each W question can be traced back to this determinant. However, the whole framework is based on context awareness, which makes this determinant extremely relevant for the whole construct, but less relevant for any single question.

(3) Boldface and italics depict entries that are important for each question and have to be taken into account when answering particular questions.

(4) Entries that are bold and in a larger font are very important for a specific ques- tion. These are crucial to take into account so that the particular question con- tributes to ubiquity.

Subsequently, the W questions to reach ubiquity within scientific entrepreneurship are answered and integrated into the ubiquitous entrepreneurship board.

5.3.2 General Framework for Ubiquitous Entrepreneurship

For ubiquitous entrepreneurship, the questions What?, Where?, Who?, When?, and Why? should be answered for the identified characteristics so that ubiquity can be reached within scientific entrepreneurship. These questions are answered in the fol- lowing five subchapters.

5.3.2.1 What Questions

Five What questions may be considered. The first three are: *What is an entrepreneurial university against the background of scientific entrepreneurship?, What is the main objective of an entrepreneurial university against the background of scientific entre- preneurship?*, and *What is needed to achieve this main objective?* Drawing upon suc- cess stories, we will see how Magin's and von Kortzfleisch's (2008) methods and in- struments can be enhanced to reach ubiquity. The last two questions are: *What are the further requirements emerging with methods and instruments?* and *What other factors must be considered?* The additional instrument of evaluation is used to answer the last question.

As discussed in subchapter 5.1, the entrepreneurial university is the key element of the second academic revolution. Hence, before ubiquity in scientific entrepreneurship is reached, each university must understand that the ongoing academic revolution promotes the entrepreneurial university, which serves as the starting point for ubiquitous entrepreneurship. Therefore, the first question each university must answer is: *What is an entrepreneurial university against the background of scientific entrepreneurship?* Although each university may have its own answer, each must consider that entrepreneurship plays a central role in developing the economy and society, according to subchapter 5.1. In addition, according to Cuevas (1994), entrepreneurship in universities can be promoted by focusing on the financial, management, and 'booster' spheres (subchapter 4.2) using specific methods and instruments (Magin and von Kortzfleisch 2008) where no method or instruments is precluded from the start.

Based on results of current research, the following entries can be made in the ubiquitous entrepreneurship board, as shown in Table 7: An entrepreneurial university, as each university defines it, promotes the three entrepreneurial spheres using certain methods and instruments according to the characteristic that nothing is precluded from the start. Answering this question is essential because each university must decide whether and how each entrepreneurial sphere influences the entrepreneurial university. As the university positions itself as entrepreneurial university, it develops a better understanding about what methods and instruments should be used to promote certain entrepreneurial spheres. Each university must find its own path to become an entrepreneurial university based on internal resources and external partners.

Table 7: Ubiquitous Entrepreneurship Board – What Question 1. (Source: Own representation.)

Question	Characteristics for ubiqutiy from ...		Entrepreneurship categorization	Ubiquitous entrepreneurship	
	Theology	IT	Entrepreneurial spheres	Entrepreneurial university	Methods and instruments +
What is an entrepreneurial university against the background of scientific entrepreneurship?	Present everywhere	Context-aware			
	Incorporeal and all-pervading	Privacy protecting			
	Immediate and localized knowledge	Collaborating	'Booster'		
	Invisible	Invisible	Financial	Individually defined	Promote entrepreneurial spheres
	Not precluding anything	Trustworthy	Management		

Next, this question can be derived: *What is the main objective of an entrepreneurial university against the background of scientific entrepreneurship?* According to Magin and von Kortzfleisch (2008, 23), successful startups begin with aspirations (see sub-chapter 5.1). Therefore, against the background of scientific entrepreneurship, the individually defined entrepreneurial university must focus on the financial, management, and booster spheres to increase the entrepreneurial education so that methods and instruments can be used to create startups that in turn develop the economy and society. Accordingly, Table 8 summarizes these results.

The next question that arises is: *What is needed to achieve this main objective?* Agan we turn to Magin's and von Kortzfleisch's (2008) work in which they describe various methods and instruments that can be successfully used to create startups. However, as with the first what question, the methods and tools must always be used to promote the financial, management, and booster spheres, which serve as basis for scientific entrepreneurship. Furthermore, other methods and instruments could conceivably be added to increase practical education at universities, according to the GEM's political implications (Sternberg et al. 2012).

Customer success stories provide examples for this enlargement. Among Germany's top 25 IT consulting and system integration companies in 2012 (Lünendonk 2013), each of the top 10 companies used customer success stories, as shown in Table 9. Thus, depending on how the entrepreneurial university is interpreted, these practical results can be transferred from industry to university to promote the entrepreneurial culture and sensitize students for each of the entrepreneurship spheres. According to Magin and von Kortzfleisch (2008, 70, 116), sensitization increases entrepreneurship perception and creates successfully startups while the entrepreneurial culture helps to remove barriers to entrepreneurship.

Table 8: Ubiquitous Entrepreneurship Board – What Question 2. (Source: Own representation.)

Question	Characteristics for ubiqutiy from ...		Entrepreneurship categorization	Ubiquitous entrepreneurship	
	Theology	IT		Entrepreneurial university	Methods and instruments +
What is the main objective of an entrepreneurial university against the background of scientific entrepreneurship?	Present everywhere	Context-aware	'Booster'	Individually defined	Sucessfully create startups to develop economics and society
	Incorporeal and all-pervading	Privacy protecting			
	Immediate and localized knowledge	Collaborating	Financial		
	Invisible	Invisible			
	Not precluding anything	Trustworthy	Management		

Table 9: Success stories in German consulting companies in 2012. (Source: Own representation.)

Companies	Success Stories		Sources*
	Yes	No	
T-Systems	X		(T-Systems 2013)
IBM Global Business Services	X		(IBM 2013)
Accenture GmbH	X		(Accenture 2013)
Capgemini Deutschland Holding GmbH	X		(Capgemini 2013)
Msg systems AG	X		(Msg systems 2007)
Atos IT GmbH / Atos Solutions & Services GmbH	X		(Atos 2013)
Allgeier SE	X		(Allgeier 2013)
Hewlett-Packard Deutschland Services	X		(Hewlett-Packard 2013)
CSC Deutschland Solutions GmbH	X		(CSC 2013)
Arvato Systems Group	X		(Arvato 2013)
Total	10/10	0/10	

* Some companies do not use a success story overview. Thus, a random link is used representatively.

On the way to achieving ubiquitous entrepreneurship no method and instrument should be excluded. In other words, as long as an entrepreneurial university promotes the three spheres of entrepreneurship to create successful startups any method and instrument can be used and nothing should be precluded. As shown in Figure 9, this claim aligns with the characteristic of ubiquity from theology: Nothing is precluded. Because Magin and von Kortzfleisch's (2008) methods and instruments are related to scientific entrepreneurship, they may need to be enlarged to reach ubiquitous entrepreneurship in academia. However, as methods and instruments are added, the three entrepreneurial spheres must be considered so that the entrepreneurial university reaches ubiquitous entrepreneurship. Recommendations for enlarging these methods and instruments follow within this subchapter.

According to Table 10, methods and instruments from scientific entrepreneurship and others that are individually defined can be used to achieve an entrepreneurial university's main objective to create startups, within the three entrepreneurial spheres.

Therefore, the next question to consider is: *What are further requirements for these methods and instruments?* Methods and instruments play an important role in scientific entrepreneurship, but to achieve ubiquity these things must be accessible and local, which mirrors the characterization of ubiquity in theology. The transfer of knowledge must occur in ways beyond lectures or classic teaching materials like slides or lecture notes. Instead, Magin and von Kortzfleisch (2008, 72) suggested that a multisensory knowledge transfer be used, especially for sensitizing students. Hence, for ubiquitous entrepreneurship, these active methods and instruments might include online business games related to entrepreneurship, embedded entrepreneurial articles in a single platform maintained by the university, or contact information of stakeholders directly related to scientific entrepreneurship, such as mentors or investors. To create immediate accessibility, online solutions are highly recommended so that potential entrepreneurs can get relevant information at any time. Because spatial proximity is also important for scientific entrepreneurship (Magin and von Kortzfleisch 2008, 35), each entrepreneurial university should establish a close network with its local stakeholders that promotes collaboration, for example, through readily available contact information for external partners. To facilitate interactions, contact information should be online so that potential entrepreneurs can proactively promote their ideas. When there is a single point of contact, these contact persons gain more experienced each time they encounter entrepreneurial ideas.

To summarize, immediate access to the methods and instruments should be ensured through the use of local knowledge to promote collaboration. This knowledge should be available to actively promote knowledge transfer between stakeholders. Table 11 summarizes these results.

Table 10: Ubiquitous Entrepreneurship Board – What Question 3. (Source: Own representation.)

Question	Characteristics for ubiquity from ...		Entrepreneurship categorization	Ubiquitous entrepreneurship
	Theology	IT	Entrepreneurial spheres	Entrepreneurial university Methods and instruments +
What is needed to achieve this main objective?	Present everywhere	Context-aware		
	Incorporeal and all-pervading	Privacy protecting	**'Booster'**	**Individually defined**
	Immediate and localized knowledge	Collaborating	**Financial**	
	Invisible	Invisible	**Management**	**Methods and instruments from scientific entrepreneurship + individually defined methods and instruments (e.g. success stories)**
	Not precluding anything	Trustworthy		

Table 11: Ubiquitous Entrepreneurship Board – What Question 4. (Source: Own representation.)

Question	Characteristics for ubiquity from ...		Entrepreneurship categorization	Ubiquitous entrepreneurship	
	Theology	IT	Entrepreneurial spheres	Entrepreneurial university	Methods and instruments +
What are further requirements coming along with methods and instruments?	Present everywhere	Context-aware		**Within individually defined entrepreneurial university and between its partners**	**Promote entrepreneurial spheres**
	Incorporeal and all-pervading	Privacy protecting			
	Immediate and localized knowledge	**Collaborating**	**'Booster'**		
	Invisible	Invisible	Financial		
	Not precluding anything	Trustworthy	Management		

However, according to the last characteristic of ubiquity in theology, local knowledge should not exclude general knowledge. For example, local banks often provide guidelines on how to write a business plan, and therefore, universities should ensure that any coursework on writing business plans corresponds with local bank requirements. However, if a local bank has very specific requirements, the university should pursue a dialogue with the bank so that the required local knowledge does not exclude general knowledge. In addition, such a dialogue would help to develop stakeholders in the local economy and society.

The final question to consider is: *What needs to be taken into consideration additionally?* At this point, privacy protection and trustworthiness, characteristics of ubiquity from are included. In addition, collaboration – the third characteristic for ubiquity in IT – is essential to reach ubiquitous entrepreneurship. However, to collaborate means that privacy protection and trustworthiness must be assured. According to Ford (2001, 4), trust is most frequently defined as *"[...] the willingness of a party to be vulnerable to the actions of another party based on the expectation that the other will perform a particular action important to the trustor, irrespective of the ability to monitor or control that other party"* (Mayer et al. 1995, 712). The mutual expectations for trust can be increased through evaluation, which complements the basic methods and instruments from Magin and von Kortzfleisch (2008). For example, stakeholders as well as investors or mentors may be evaluated so that others are able to form an opinion based on the results. The same applies to material infrastructure like working areas. Based on evaluations, expectations are steered toward a certain direction, trust can be supported, and the evaluation results can be used to improve material infrastructure and/or stakeholder collaboration. Of course, privacy protections also influence trust.

The main objective of scientific entrepreneurship is a successful startup, and these startups need to have their innovations protected. Hence, privacy protection plays a major role in reaching entrepreneurship's ubiquity, and is the second most frequently identified characteristic of ubiquity in IT. Two areas are particularly relevant for privacy protection. First, the university and its potential entrepreneurs must ensure that privacy is protected through contracts. Even though investors may reject a business plan, the owner's idea must still be protected so that another party cannot use it. Therefore, contracts supporting privacy protection are very important for ubiquitous entrepreneurship and (ideally) are provided from the entrepreneurial university. Second, a virtual community with digital data processing is one of the main instruments used in scientific entrepreneurship (Magin and von Kortzfleisch 2008, 100), and therefore, internal resources must be used to protect privacy. Whenever methods and instruments include digital processed personal data, the data protection official must evaluate the solution to ensure that privacy is protected, which is mandated by the German Federal Data Protection Act, Section 4f.[47]

To summarize, Table 12 shows that evaluations and a protection official should be used within the entrepreneurial university and between its partners to ensure privacy protection and trustworthiness. These methods protect innovation in the booster sphere, help create necessary capital in the financial sphere, and help to organize the startup process in the management sphere.

---

[47] Cf. Federal Data Protection Act (BDSG) in the version promulgated on 14 January 2003 (Federal Law Gazette I, p. 66), last amended by Article 1 of the Act of 14 August 2009 (Federal Law Gazette I, p. 2814), in force from 1 September 2009.

Table 12: Ubiquitous Entrepreneurship Board – What Question 5. (Source: Own representation.)

Question	Characteristics for ubiquitiy from ...		Entrepreneurship categorization	Ubiquitous entrepreneurship
	Theology	IT		
What needs to be taken into consideration additionally?	Present everywhere	Context-aware	Entrepreneurial spheres	Entrepreneurial university
	Incorporeal and all-pervading	**Privacy protecting**	**'Booster'**	Methods and instruments +
	Immediate and localized knowledge	Collaborating	**Financial**	Within individually defined entrepreneurial university and between its partners
	Invisible	Invisible	**Management**	Any method and instrument (especially evaluation and the data protection official)
	Not precluding anything	**Trustworthy**		

5.3.2.2 Where Question

This subchapter takes up the question *Where should scientific entrepreneurship be available?*, and contains a proposal for enhancing methods and instruments from Magin and von Kortzfleisch (2008) with a unified content strategy to steer the information flow within the entrepreneurial university.

Against the background of reaching ubiquity and based on the most frequently mentioned characteristic of ubiquity from theology, the answer to the where question is everywhere. Scientific entrepreneurship with its methods and instruments has to be present everywhere to pervade the whole university and attract external stakeholders like investors or mentors. Only then can ubiquity in scientific entrepreneurship be reached.

But what is meant by everywhere? Of course, everywhere includes the entrepreneurial university and its third parties. Usually, the universities' organization consists of the university board, including the president, vice president, chancellor, and the presidium. Furthermore, committees like the senate or the university council can be found. Finally, universities also have faculties and deans, as well as students, student organizations, computer centers, lecturers, and university administrations. All of these must know how their particular university defines entrepreneurship and why the methods and instruments of scientific entrepreneurship are important because this knowledge will help to form a close collaboration.

Scientific entrepreneurship and its methods and instruments should be everywhere in a way that the whole university is pervaded with entrepreneurship. Therefore, it is important to use approaches that allow the university to steer, target, and manage information. Rockley and Cooper's (2012) industry approach to content management enterprise strategies are applicable to universities. They proposed a unified content strategy that identifies the content lifecycle, which consists of content creation, content review, content management, and content delivery (89). Applying this idea to the entrepreneurial university would effectively increase collaboration within the university, beginning with entrepreneurial content creation and ending with entrepreneurial content delivery, as stakeholders work closely together to promote scientific entrepreneurship. For example, if lecturers who specialize in one or more entrepreneurial sphere(s), propose action items regarding scientific entrepreneurship to the university board, an all-pervading entrepreneurial strategy may be derived and may filter down so that all university stakeholders get the right information in the right form. As a result, the whole university is systematically pervaded with scientific entrepreneurship. Additionally, the coordinated response to the action items may increase if external partners are involved in the decision-making process as soon as possible to establish a close collaboration.

To conclude, each entrepreneurial university must develop a certain strategy to promote scientific entrepreneurship within the entire university including its external partners, and close collaboration seems to be the key to success. As shown in Table 13, a content management strategy can be chosen to make entrepreneurship present everywhere and to increase the transparency of the information flow within the university and among its partners. In the end, scientific entrepreneurship pervades the entrepreneurial university, which impacts the entrepreneurial spheres that create innovation, provide capital, and organize successful startups.

Table 13: Ubiquitous Entrepreneurship Board – Where Question. (Source: Own representation.)

Question	Characteristics for ubiquity from ...		Entrepreneurship categorization	Ubiquitous entrepreneurship	
	Theology	IT	Entrepreneurial spheres	Entrepreneurial university	Methods and instruments +
Where should scientific entrepreneurship be available?	**Present everywhere**	Context-aware		**Within individually defined entrepreneurial university and between its partners**	**Any method and instrument (in particular content management strategy)**
	Incorporeal and **all-pervading**	Privacy protecting	*'Booster'*		
	Immediate and localized knowledge	**Collaborating**	*Financial*		
	Invisible	Invisible	*Management*		
	Not precluding anything	Trustworthy			

5.3.2.3 Who Question

This subchapter considers the question: *Who is affected by scientific entrepreneurship?*

As discussed, collaboration within the university may increase if the methods and instruments for scientific entrepreneurship are available within the whole university and emphasize the importance of each entrepreneurial sphere. Therefore, lecturers, students, and administration employees should be aware of these methods and instruments as well, and as stated, the methods and instruments from Magin and von Kortzfleisch (2008) can be extended as necessary to address certain stakeholders. However, collaboration does not end within the university, but should be closely established with local third parties and should be paired with a network to contact persons.

Table 14 summarizes how the entrepreneurial university's employees and partners are affected by scientific entrepreneurship. In addition, parties should not be considered separately because only collaboration promotes scientific entrepreneurship and increases its ubiquity.

Table 14: Ubiquitous Entrepreneurship Board – Who Question. (Source: Own representation.)

Question	Characteristics for ubiquity from ...		Entrepreneurship categorization	Ubiquitous entrepreneurship	
	Theology	IT	Entrepreneurial spheres	Entrepreneurial university	Methods and instruments +
Who is affected by scientific entrepreneurship?	Present everywhere	Context-aware		Entrepreneurial university's employees and students as well as local external partners	Any method and instrument
	Incorporeal and all-pervading	Privacy protecting	'Booster'		
	Immediate and localized knowledge	Collaborating	Financial		
	Invisible	Invisible	Management		
	Not precluding anything	Trustworthy			

5.3.2.4 When Question

This subchapter answers the question: *When should the methods and instruments be used?*, and introduces a new instrument, the entrepreneurial certificate, to promote ubiquitous entrepreneurship. As discussed, a close collaboration within the entrepreneurial university is required to reach ubiquitous entrepreneurship, and this collaboration can be used to control when certain methods and tools are most useful. For example, the curriculum can be steered when certain methods and instruments are applied to lectures and exercises. However, if the curriculum cannot be or should not be adapted, an "entrepreneurship certificate" may be introduced to reach ubiquitous entrepreneurship. For example, the University of Applied Sciences Hochschule Harz uses the so-called "Atos-Siemens-Certificate"[48] through which students attain additional qualifications in Enterprise Resource Planning (ERP) systems (Scheruhn 2013). Students choose from specified subjects, fulfill certain requirements, and are awarded the certificate that signifies their additional knowledge in a specific field of research. This idea can be adopted to improve entrepreneurship education within universities. Instead of changing the curriculum, the entrepreneurial certificate's structure can be used to guide potential entrepreneurs through coursework that focuses on the three entrepreneurial spheres and provides them additional qualifications in scientific entrepreneurship for creating startups. Compared with curriculum changes, a certificate program may be an easier method to motivate potential entrepreneurs to acquire additional knowledge and guide them through the entrepreneurial education.

As noted, methods and instruments must be available immediately and everywhere. Therefore, methods and instruments may be considered predefined – such as a curriculum or certificate – or dynamic – such as immediate access to the necessary tools that an entrepreneur may need to start an innovative business. Additionally, time is as important a factor to reach ubiquity entrepreneurship as it is in IT. For example, Abowd and Mynatt (2000) identified a new area in ubiquitous computing – called everyday computing – in which interactions are scaled with respect to time. Within entrepre-

---

[48] The certificate originally was founded by Siemens IT Solutions and Services GmbH, but because Atos, an international IT services company, acquired Siemens IT Solutions and Services GmbH in 2011 (Atos 2011) both companies are named within this certificate.

neurship, Bruyat and Julien (2000, 168) noted that entrepreneurship also must considered time. Finally, as discussed in subchapter 5.2, time is a key element in the process-oriented approach (Magin and von Kortzfleisch 2008, 14). Therefore ubiquitous entrepreneurship requires providing methods and instruments in a timely predefined, dynamic way.

Table 15 summarizes the answer to the when question. As shown, immediate access to the methods and instruments are recommended to reach ubiquity in scientific entrepreneurship, and online solutions may be the best means to achieve immediacy. The majority of Magin and von Kortzfleisch's (2008) methods and instruments can be used online, for example, lectures, questionnaires for self-assessments, room allocation plans, or multiplayer business games. Additionally, the suggested enlargements also can be available online, such as success stories, the entrepreneurship certificate, or evaluations. Besides these dynamic tools, collaboration can lead to a predefined certificate or curriculum. A close collaboration among lecturers, especially who address the entrepreneurial sphere(s), may help to guide potential entrepreneurs through the entrepreneurial education with a predefined, time-schedule offering, when certain methods and instruments are used. However, potential entrepreneurs should always be able to access the methods and instruments immediately for a quick, successful startup.

Table 15: Ubiquitous Entrepreneurship Board – When Question. (Source: Own representation.)

Question	Characteristics for ubiquity from ...		Entrepreneurship categorization	Ubiquitous entrepreneurship	
	Theology	IT	Entrepreneurial spheres	Entrepreneurial university	Methods and instruments +
When should the methods and instruments be used?	Present everywhere	Context-aware	'Booster'		**Dynamically with immediate access or pre-defined in terms of curriculum or "entrepreneurship certificate"**
	Incorporeal and all-pervading	Privacy protecting	Financial	Individually defined	
	Immediate and localized knowledge	**Collaborating**	Management		
	Invisible	Invisible			
	Not precluding anything	Trustworthy			

5.3.2.5 Why Questions

Finally, three why questions must be answered in order to reach ubiquitous entrepreneurship: *Why is ubiquitous scientific entrepreneurship important for the university?*, *Why does scientific entrepreneurship need to be visible?* and *Why is scientific entrepreneurship corporeal?*

First, the question, *why is ubiquitous scientific entrepreneurship important for the university?*, entails that the entrepreneurial university consider the benefits of scientific entrepreneurship. As discussed in subchapter 5.1, Etzkowitz (2003, 110) stated that these benefits are economic and social development. Furthermore, as subchapter 4.3 highlighted, the university is the ideal starting point for entrepreneurship to create economic growth. Hence, the promotion of scientific entrepreneurship not only develops the economy and society, it also may create a new revenue source for the entrepreneurial university. If a university focuses on scientific entrepreneurship and becomes an entrepreneurial university, the chances of generating successful startups increase. Because the university offers infrastructure and knowledge, over time successful startups may possibly support the university financially through newly introduced method of refinancing. When entrepreneurship plays a ubiquitous role within the university, its advantages will be transferred to third parties, such as investors, who also will understand entrepreneurship's benefits. As a result, these third parties will understand that good ideas lead to successful startups and profit creation, which finally will pay off previous investments.

Table 16 highlights how the entrepreneurial university benefits from scientific entrepreneurship, and therefore, from successful startup creations that develop the economy and society. The better the three entrepreneurial spheres are promoted, the better the opportunity to benefit from this entrepreneurial education. Primarily, the university may benefit from financial support so that prior efforts in education pay off. The method of refinancing increases the university's room to maneuver for future investments that promote scientific entrepreneurship. Secondarily, collaboration for ubiquitous scientific entrepreneurship remains important. If all employees of the university and their partners move closer together, a better knowledge exchange may result, and potential may be better utilized. Additionally, the university's proverbial "ivory tower mentality," which considers research as the only mission to the exclusion of economic and societal effects, gradually disappears. Therefore, ubiquitous scientific entrepreneurship is also important for universities because it is the prerequisite for Viale and Etzkowitz's (2005, 2) third academic revolution, in which the entrepreneurial university is the center of a society's knowledge creation and knowledge diffusion. For this reason, the entrepreneurial university is well positioned to response to future challenges, too.

The second why question concerns invisibility: *Why does scientific entrepreneurship need to be visible?* A visible scientific entrepreneurship differs from the characteristics of ubiquity in theology and IT, which emphasize invisibility: In theology, God is invisible because God is incorporeal and intangible, and in ubiquitous computing, technology disappears into the background so that humans are not bothered by it. But to reach ubiquitous entrepreneurship, a different strategy should be used: Methods and instruments should make scientific entrepreneurship as present and as visible as possible within an entrepreneurial university so that everyone encounters it. For instance, the Ludwig Maximilian University in Munich has an entrepreneurship center with the clear mission: "Empowering Entrepreneurs!" and scientific entrepreneurship is visible through teaching, research, labs, and communities throughout the entire university and for its partners (Ludwig Maximilian University 2013). Finally, this visibility can be used to create an entrepreneurial culture and a corporate identity (Capriotti 2009, 228) because the "we are an entrepreneurial university feeling" emphasizes the university's "corporate brand" of entrepreneurship, similar to companies with a strong corporate identity like Apple or Nike (Franzen and Moriarty 2009, 400).

Table 17 summarizes these results. Scientific entrepreneurship must be as visible as possible to ensure that the booster, financial, and management spheres are promoted optimally, especially with methods and instruments that affect the entrepreneurial culture and bolster the entrepreneurial university's corporate identity.

Table 16: Ubiquitous Entrepreneurship Board – Why Question 1. (Source: Own representation.)

Question	Characteristics for ubiquity from ...		Entrepreneurship categorization	Ubiquitous entrepreneurship	
	Theology	IT	Entrepreneurial spheres	Entrepreneurial university	Methods and instruments +
Why is ubiquitous scientific entrepreneurship important for the university?	Present everywhere	Context-aware			
	Incorporeal and all-pervading	Privacy protecting	'Booster'		
	Immediate and localized knowledge	Collaborating	Financial	Benefits from economic and social development	Especially refinancing
	Invisible	Invisible	Management		
	Not precluding anything	Trustworthy			

Table 17: Ubiquitous Entrepreneurship Board – Why Question 2. (Source: Own representation.)

Question	Characteristics for ubiquity from ...		Entrepreneurship categorization	Ubiquitous entrepreneurship
	Theology	IT		
	Present everywhere	Context-aware	Entrepreneurial spheres	Entrepreneurial university
	Incorporeal and all-pervading	Privacy protecting	'Booster'	Methods and instruments +
Why does scientific entrepreneurship need to be visible?	Immediate and localized knowledge	Collaborating	Financial	Individually defined
	Visible	**Visible**	**Management**	**Promote entrepreneurial spheres especially with entrepreneurial culture and corporate identity to make them as visible as possible**
	Not precluding anything	Trustworthy		

Finally, a question regarding incorporeality must be addressed: *Why is scientific entrepreneurship corporeal?* Similar to the previous question, this one also reverses the incorporeal characteristic of ubiquity in theology. In scientific entrepreneurship, methods and instruments should be as tangible as possible. In addition, genuine partnerships, demonstrated with success stories, and the design-thinking method literally make entrepreneurship corporeal. An innovative product or service is created step by step, starting with an idea for how to solve a problem, followed by prototyping, and ending with the realization (Hasso-Plattner-Institut 2013). Therefore, design thinking visualizes innovation especially before the realization process starts. Obviously, design thinking is primarily related to the booster sphere (see subchapter 4.2). Nevertheless, other spheres also must be corporeal. For example, in the financial sphere, third parties may be invited to the university to talk about entrepreneurial failures and successes, and in the management sphere, former researchers who started a business may be invited to talk about their experiences. In this way, these experts help to embody a certain sphere so that scientific entrepreneurship becomes corporeal and inspires current researchers with these experiences.

Table 18 summarizes the answer to this third why question. The methods and instruments used within the entrepreneurial university should promote the three entrepreneurial spheres so that scientific entrepreneurship becomes corporeal. According to the table, making the booster sphere as corporeal as possible is most important because innovation is created at that stage, although corporeality is important for the other spheres, too, and reasonable efforts should be made to make them corporeal.

Table 18: Ubiquitous Entrepreneurship Board – Why Question 3. (Source: Own representation.)

Question	Characteristics for ubiquity from ...		Entrepreneurship categorization	Ubiquitous entrepreneurship
	Theology	IT		
Why is scientific entrepreneurship corporeal?	Present everywhere	Context-aware	Entrepreneurial spheres	Entrepreneurial university
	Corporeal and all-pervading	Privacy protecting	**'Booster'**	Methods and instruments +
	Immediate and localized knowledge	Collaborating	*Financial*	Individually defined
	Invisible	Invisible	*Management*	
	Not precluding anything	Trustworthy		Promote entrepreneurial spheres to become as corporeal as possible

5.3.3 Summary of the Framework

According to Figure 11, the individually defined entrepreneurial university, with its innovative booster sphere, profit-oriented financial sphere, and supervision-oriented management sphere, promotes scientific entrepreneurship with the help of certain methods and instruments. Therefore, these parts play key roles within the framework and individually define each university as entrepreneurial. To make scientific entrepreneurship ubiquitous within the entrepreneurial university, the framework uses context awareness as a basic determinant. Accordingly, the five Ws – What?, Where?, Who?, When?, and Why? – must be answered. As Figure 11 shows, the what questions define ubiquitous scientific entrepreneurship so that nothing is precluded from the start, especially regarding selection, usage, and enhancement of methods and instruments that the individually defined entrepreneurial university may apply within the three entrepreneurial spheres. Moreover, the methods and instruments must be accessible immediately, and external partners' knowledge also must be tapped. Thus, close collaborations within the entrepreneurial university and between the university and its local partners are mandatory to reach ubiquitous entrepreneurship. Finally, trust is the common bond that increases collaboration and privacy protection ensures open collaboration. The where question points out the necessity for scientific entrepreneurship to be present everywhere and for sustainable ubiquitous entrepreneurship to pervade the entrepreneurial university and its local partners. Hence, a close collaboration is a prerequisite here, too. Regarding the who question, again collaboration is important to make scientific entrepreneurship ubiquitous because the methods and instruments affect the employees of the entrepreneurial university and external. The better the collaboration, the better the outcome will be for both the entrepreneurial university and its partners. Furthermore, two different perspectives guide when to uses certain methods to promote ubiquitous entrepreneurship: Online solutions provide relevant information that is immediately available, and collaboration with external partners provides examples of practical applications to guide potential entrepreneurs through the entrepreneurial education within the university. With the why questions, collaboration increases practical education and may reduce the university's "ivory tower mentality," paving the way for a third academic revolution (Viale and Etzkowitz 2005, 2).

Besides, the entrepreneurial university must make entrepreneurship as visible and as corporeal as possible to form a corporate identity and to ensure that potential entrepreneurs encounter scientific entrepreneurship as often as possible.

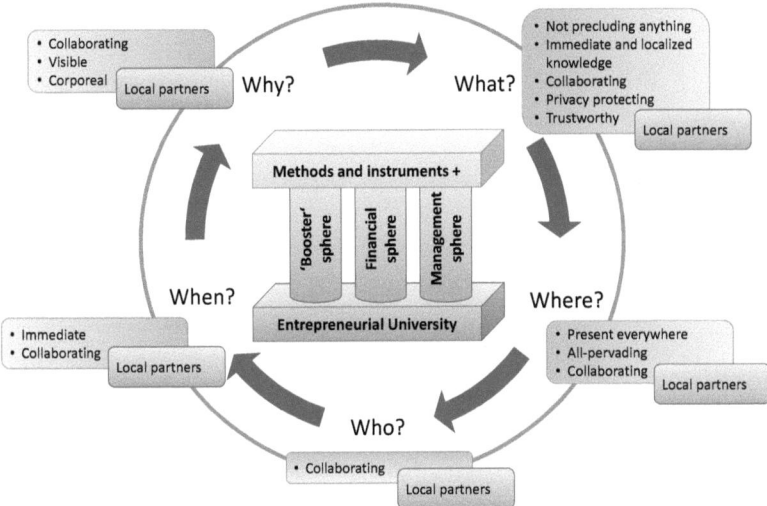

Figure 11: General framework with assigned determinants from humanities and IT. (Source: Own representation.)

Finally, Figure 11 indicates that that *collaboration* is relevant for each question. Therefore, *local partners* are very important to reach ubiquitous entrepreneurship. Hence, the close collaboration between each entrepreneurial university and its local partners reflects GEM's political demand that an increased practical education in universities will to strengthen the knowledge and technology transfer between universities and industry (Sternberg et al. 2012, 25).

6 Conclusion

This final chapter summarizes the results and highlights this book's contribution to theory: the characterization of ubiquity and the transfer of these characteristics to scientific entrepreneurship to reach ubiquity within this field of research (subchapter 6.1). Moreover, this book also contributes to practice because the suggested Ubiquitous Entrepreneurship Board can be used to increase practical feasibility. Subchapter 6.2 identifies further research that is needed, especially regarding the practical feasibility, the digitalization of the general framework and the Ubiquitous Entrepreneurship Board, and continual developments in the field of IT.

6.1 Summary of the Results

The main goal of this book is to emphasize the impact of theology and IT on ubiquitous scientific entrepreneurship and to promote practical ways to make scientific entrepreneurship ubiquitous within universities in order to create more startups, for economic and societal benefit. Therefore, three research questions were addressed. The first, *What are the characteristics for ubiquity in humanities?*, arises from the etymology of the term ubiquity, which indicates that God is considered omnipresent. Within theology, 14 sources were identified that explored God's ubiquity in three major religions – Christianity, Islam, and Hinduism – and these characteristics were listed: God is present everywhere, God is incorporeal and all-pervading, God has immediate and localized knowledge, God is invisible, and finally, God does not precluding anything. Moreover, in the field of law, ubiquity occurs as legal ubiquity and as the principle of ubiquity. The first is a temporary phenomenon that attributes godlike characteristics to the king, and the latter is considered a figure of speech within jurisprudence. These characteristics of ubiquity in law were eliminated as being insignificant for this book's discussions.

In addition to characteristics from the mainly history-oriented humanities, characteristics from the future-oriented field of IT also were investigated, especially regarding ubiquitous computing. Thus, characteristics of ubiquity were derived from a second perspective, which allowed consideration of current research trends. Hence, the second research question, *What are the characteristics for ubiquity in IT?*, can be answered as follows: Similar to the humanities research, 14 sources were identified for research in IT, and characteristics of ubiquity were identified, including context aware, privacy protecting, collaborating, invisible (also in theology), and trustworthy.

To answer the third research question – *How can characteristics from humanities and IT enable ubiquitous entrepreneurship?* – entrepreneurship first had to be defined. Several theories regarding entrepreneurship were highlighted, which describe entrepreneurship differently because entrepreneurship means different things to different people. Thus, a uniform definition does not exist. However, instead of developing a limited definition, Cuevas' (1994) holistic approach was selected, which derives three spheres out of the investigated entrepreneurship theories. Therefore, entrepreneurship was categorized according to the innovative and risk-oriented booster sphere, the profit-oriented financial sphere, and finally, the supervision-oriented management sphere.

Current EU entrepreneurship projects demonstrate that entrepreneurship can be promoted through education. To understand why entrepreneurship should be promoted within today's universities, the book summarized the historical development of the university's missions: initially teaching, then research, and currently the focus on entrepreneurship. A distinction was made between academic entrepreneurship – the institutional view – and scientific entrepreneurship – the functional view – using an engineering approach with methods and instruments. The action fields of the engineering approach to entrepreneurship, which Magin and von Kortzfleisch (2008) called scientific entrepreneurship engineering, can be assigned to Cuevas' (1994) three entrepreneurial spheres. Therefore, the key to ubiquitous scientific entrepreneurship is using the methods and instruments of each action field ubiquitously to promote the three entrepreneurial spheres, a process that characterizes the entrepreneurial university and makes scientific entrepreneurship sustainably ubiquitous in universities.

As a result, the third research question was be answered as follows: Ubiquitous scientific entrepreneurship can be enabled by applying the developed framework, which uses the identified characteristics of ubiquity from humanities and IT. The general framework positions the entrepreneurial university and its relevant methods and instruments with the booster, financial, and management spheres in the center. Around this are depiction are the five W questions that must be answered to provide context awareness, the most frequently determined characteristic for ubiquity within IT. Answers to the what questions establishes basis for ubiquitous entrepreneurship within the entrepreneurial university. As a result, nothing is precluding, which provides the highest flexibility to reach ubiquitous scientific entrepreneurship for each entrepreneurial university. Furthermore, close collaboration within the university and between the university and local partners ensures immediate access to localized knowledge. Moreover, the collaboration must be based on trustworthiness and privacy protection.

The question concerning where the methods and instruments are used was answered by making them present everywhere so entrepreneurship pervades both the entrepreneurial university and its local partners, based on close collaboration. Thus, the answer to who is affected by scientific entrepreneurship is the university and its partners, and the collaboration between them is most important especially to increase the practicality of education.

As to when to use methods and instruments to promote scientific entrepreneurship, immediate access must be ensured to provide the greatest flexibility to potential entrepreneurs and a predefined path through the entrepreneurial education also should available to provide an entrepreneurial education according to the three entrepreneurial spheres. Hence, this approach combines flexibility and guidance.

Finally, answers to the why questions pointed out that entrepreneurship is essential for today's universities and may create new revenue streams. Furthermore, scientific entrepreneurship can be ubiquitous only if it is corporeal and visible, traits that create a corporate identity to prove that scientific entrepreneurship is successful.

After each of the questions have been answered, the entrepreneurial university must process the framework again to continuously improve its actions.

Besides the general framework, the Ubiquitous Entrepreneurship Board increases the model's practical feasibility. This model was developed to ensure that each university can use the identified characteristics for ubiquity from theology and IT to individually define itself as an entrepreneurial university, based on the three entrepreneurial spheres, and derive methods and instruments to promote ubiquitous entrepreneurship holistically. Therefore, this book contributes to theory through its characterization of both ubiquity and entrepreneurship and contributes to practice through the Ubiquitous Entrepreneurship Board, which can be used as strategic guideline for the practical feasibility of ubiquitous scientific entrepreneurship.

6.2 Further Research Needs

The book is pioneering in its theoretical characterization of ubiquity and its practical model for implementation of ubiquitous scientific entrepreneurship using the developed framework. However, future research is needed in several areas. First, the practical feasibility of the general framework and of the Ubiquitous Entrepreneurship Board should be tested to identify potential deficits. Experiences with these models are needed to determine whether the framework based on the five Ws is sufficient. At this point, key performance indicators may need to be defined to measure how ubiquity is reached.

Second, the general framework and the Ubiquitous Entrepreneurship Board should be digitalized to ensure immediate data access and data exchange. It may be technically feasible for the Ubiquitous Entrepreneurship Board to serve as a scorecard for each entrepreneurial university to determine its strengths and weaknesses. Based on the results, partner universities could be identified. For example, a university with strengths in the management and the financial spheres could cooperate with one having strengths in the booster sphere so that both universities can advance.

Third, ubiquitous computing is a relatively new research area that is still developing. Further changes are likely. For example, Google's project Glass (Google 2013), which uses glasses as a head-up display, takes the embeddedness and mobility of ubiquitous computing to a new level. Therefore, this development – and others – must be considered to derive impacts such as possible privacy violations, and transfer these factors to ubiquitous entrepreneurship. Finally, research in IT, and especially in ubiquitous computing, must be analyzed again in the near future to validate the identified characteristics.

References

3 Day Startup. 2013. "3 Day Startup – About Us." Accessed April 19, 2013. http://3daystartup.org/about/.

Abowd, G. D., and E. D. Mynatt. 2000. "Charting Past, Present, and Future Research in Ubiquitous Computing." *ACM Transactions on Computer-Human Interaction* 7 (1): 29–58.

Accenture. 2013. "Bayerischer Rundfunk – Steigerung der Effizienz der Personalarbeit." Accessed August 18, 2013. http://www.accenture.com/de-de/Pages/success-bayerischer-personalarbeit.aspx.

Ahamed, S. V. 2007. *English Translation of the Message of the Quran*. 3rd ed. Lombard, IL: Book of Signs Foundation.

Allgeier, 2013. "Referenzen & Case Studies." Accessed August 18, 2013. http://www.allgeier-holding.de/de/pressroom/references.

Anagnostopoulos, C. B., A. Tsounis, and S. Hadjiefthymiades. 2007. "Context Awareness in Mobile Computing Environments." *Wireless Personal Communications* 42 (3): 445–464.

Anderson, A. R., and M. Starnawska. 2008. "Research Practices in Entrepreneurship: Problems of Definition, Description and Meaning." *International Journal of Entrepreneurship and Innovation* 9 (4): 221–230.

Arvato, 2013. "Expertise for Numerous Industries and Business Processes." Accessed August 18, 2013. http://www.arvato-systems.de/com/customers.html.

Ashmore, C. 2005. *Entrepreneurship Everywhere: The Case for Entrepreneurship Education*. Columbus, OH: The Consortium for Entrepreneurship Education.

Atkinson, A. B., E. Marlier, and B. Nolan. 2004. "Indicators and Targets for Social Inclusion in the European Union." *Journal of Common Market Studies* 42 (1): 47–75.

Atos. 2011. "Atos and Siemens have finalized the acquisition by Atos of Siemens IT Solutions and Services." Accessed July 10, 2013. http://atos.net/en-us/home/we-are/news/press-release/2011/pr-2011_07_01_01.html.

Atos. 2013. "Unsere Kunden." Accessed August 18, 2013. http://de.atos.net/de-de/uber_uns/unsere-kunden/default.htm.

Attewell, P. 1992. "Technology Diffusion and Organizational Learning: The Case of Business Computing." *Organization Science* 3 (1): 1–19.

Audretsch, D. B. 2007. "Entrepreneurship Capital and Economic Growth." *Oxford Review of Economic Policy* 23 (1): 63–78.

Barnard, L. W. 1964. "Clement of Rome and the Persecution of Domitian." *New Testament Studies* 10 (2): 251–260.

Berman, H. J. 1994. "The Origins of Historical Jurisprudence: Coke, Selden, Hale." *The Yale Law Journal* 103 (7): 1651–1738.

Bertilsson, M. 1992. "From University to Comprehensive Higher Education: On the Widening Gap Between 'Lehre und Leben.'" *Higher Education* 24 (3): 333–349.

Bible Gateway Online. 1995. s. v. "God's Omnipresence and Omniscience." Accessed April 22, 2013. http://www.biblegateway.com/passage/?search=Psalm+139&version=NASB#fen-NASB-16248f.

Bible Gateway Online. 2013. s. v. *New American Standard Bible (NASB).* Accessed April 22, 2013. Available at: http://www.biblegateway.com/versions/New-American-Standard-Bible-NASB/.

Blackstone, W. 1765. *Commentaries On The Laws Of England. Book the First.* Oxford: Clarendon Press.

Blackstone, W. 1979. *Commentaries on the Laws of England, Volume 4: A Facsimile of the First Edition of 1765–1769.* Chicago: University of Chicago Press.

Bolt, G., J. Burgers, and R. Van Kempen. 1998. "On the Social Significance of Spatial Location: Spatial Segregation and Social Inclusion." *Netherlands Journal of Housing and the Built Environment* 13: 83–95.

Braunerhjelm, P. 2007. "Academic Entrepreneurship: Social Norms, University Culture and Policies." *Science and Public Policy* 34 (9): 619–631.

Bravo, J., R. Hervás, and G. Chavira. 2005. "Ubiquitous Computing in the Classroom: An Approach through Identification Process." *Journal of Universal Computer Science* 11 (9): 1494–1504.

Brooks, K. 2003. "The Context Quintet: Narrative Elements Applied to Context Awareness." Proceedings of the Human Computer Interaction International.

Bruyat, C. and P.-A. Julien. 2000. "Defining the Field of Research in Entrepreneurship." *Journal of Business Venturing* 16: 165–180.

Bull, I. and G. E. Willard. 1993. "Towards a Theory of Entrepreneurship. *"Journal of Business Venturing* 8: 183–195.

Bull, I., G. Willard, and H. C. Thomas. 1995. *Entrepreneurship: Perspectives on Theory Building.* Oxford: Pergamon.

Butler, E. 2010. *Ludwig von Mises – A Primer.* London: The Institute of Economic Affairs.

Capgemini. 2013. "Kundenreferenzen." Accessed August 18, 2013. http://www.de.capgemini.com/kunden.

Capriotti, P. 2009. "Economic and Social Roles of Companies in the Mass Media: The Impact Media Visibility Has on Businesses' Being Recognized as Economic and Social Actors." *Business Society* 48 (2): 225–242.

Christian Classics Ethereal Library. 2013. *Biography of St. Anselm.* Accessed April 19, 2013. http://www.ccel.org/ccel/anselm.

Coase, R. H. 1937. "The Nature of the Firm." *Economica* 4 (16): 386–405.

Collins English Dictionary Online. 2009. s. v. "ubiquity." Accessed February 26, 2013. http://dictionary.reference.com/browse/ubiquity

Costa, M. 2008. "The Omnipresence of God in the View of Strong and Panneberg Compared to a Biblical Analysis." *Hermenêutica* 8: 85–109.

Cranz, F. E. 1950. "De Civitate Dei, XV, 2, and Augustine's Idea of the Christian Society." *Speculum* 25 (2): 215–225.

CSC. 2013. "Success Stories." Accessed August 18, 2013. http://www.csc.com/de/success_stories.

Cuevas, J. G. 1994. "Towards a Taxonomy of Entrepreneurial Theories." *International Small Business Journal* 12: 77–88.

Desikan, P. et al. 2009. "Web Mining for Business Computing." In *Business Computing,* edited by G. Adomavicius and A. Gupta, 45–68. Bingley, UK: Emerald Group Publishing.

Dey, A. K., G. D. Abowd, and D. Salber. 2001. "A Conceptual Framework and a Toolkit for Supporting the Rapid Prototyping of Context-Aware Applications." *Human-Computer Interaction* 16 (2–4): 97–166.

Dictionary.com. 2013. s. v. "ubiquity." Accessed February 26, 2013. http://dictionary.reference.com/browse/ubiquity.

Dyck, G. M. 1977. "Omnipresence and Incorporeality." *Religious Studies* 13: 85–91.

Eltis, W. A. 1975. "Francois Quesnay: A Reinterpretation – 1. The Tableau Economique." *Oxford Economic Papers* 27 (2): 167–200.

Elwell, W. A. 2001. *Evangelical Dictionary of Theology,* 2nd ed. Grand Rapids, MI: Baker Academic.

Encyclopædia Britannica Online. 2013. s. v. "Paul-Émile Littré." Accessed April 4, 2013. http://www.britannica.com/EBchecked/topic/344289/Paul-Emile-Littre.

Etzkowitz, H. 1998. "The Norms of Entrepreneurial Science: Cognitive Effects of the New University – Industry Linkages." *Research Policy* 27: 823–833.

Etzkowitz, H. 2002. *MIT and the Rise of Entrepreneurial Science*. London, New York: Routledge.

Etzkowitz, H. 2003. "Innovation in Innovation: The Triple Helix of University-Industry-Government Relations." *Social Science Information* 42 (3): 293–337.

Etzkowitz, H. 2003. "Research Groups as 'Quasi-Firms': The Invention of the Entrepreneurial University." *Research Policy* 32 (1): 109–121.

Etzkowitz, H., and L. Leydesdorff. 2000. "The Dynamics of Innovation: From National Systems and 'Mode 2' to a Triple Helix of University-Industry-Government Relations." *Research Policy* 29 (2): 109–123.

Etzkowitz, H., A. Webster, C. Gebhardt, and B. R. C. Terra. 2000. "The Future of the University and the University of the Future: Evolution of Ivory Tower to Entrepreneurial Paradigm." *Research Policy* 29 (2): 313–330.

Etzkowitz, H., A. Webster, and P. Healey. 1998. *Capitalizing Knowledge – New Intersections of Industry and Academia*. New York: SUNY Press.

European Commission. 2010a. *Lisbon Strategy Evaluation Document*. Brussels: European Commission.

European Commission. 2010b. *Europe 2020*. Brussels: European Commission.

European Commission. 2012. *Effects and Impact of Entrepreneurship Programmes in Higher Education*. Brussels: Entrepreneurship Unit.

European Commission. 2013a. "Competitiveness and Innovation Framework Programme (CIP)." Accessed June 18, 2013. http://ec.europa.eu/cip/index_en.htm.

European Commission. 2013b. "Promotion of Entrepreneurship." Accessed June 18, 2013. http://ec.europa.eu/cip/eip/promotion-entrepreneurship/index_en.htm.

European Commission. 2013c. "Programme for the Competitiveness of Enterprises and SMEs (COSME) 2014–2020." Accessed June 18, 2013. http://ec.europa.eu/cip/cosme/index_en.htm.

European Commission. 2013d. "Small and Medium-Sized Enterprises (SMEs) –
Entrepreneurship 2020 Action Plan." Accessed June 18, 2013.
http://ec.europa.eu/enterprise/policies/sme/entrepreneurship-2020/index_en.htm.

European Commission. 2013e. "Small and Medium-Sized Enterprises (SMEs) –
Promoting Entrepreneurship." Accessed June 19, 2013.
http://ec.europa.eu/enterprise/policies/sme/promoting-
entrepreneurship/index_en.htm.

European Foundation for Entrepreneurship Research. 2006. *20 Centers of Dynamic
Entrepreneurship.* Munich: EFER.

Fahlbusch, E. et al. 1999. *The Encyclopedia of Christianity,* 2nd ed. Grand Rapids, MI:
William B. Eerdmans Publishing.

Fano, A., and A. Gershman. 2002. "The Future of Business Services in the Age of
Ubiquitous Computing." *Communications of the ACM* 45 (12): 83–87.

Federal Communications Commission. 2013. "What We Do." Accessed April 23, 2013.
http://www.fcc.gov/what-we-do.

Federal Ministry of Economics and Technology (BMWi). 2013a. "EXIST –
Existenzgründungen aus der Wissenschaft." Accessed June 18, 2013.
http://www.exist.de/exist/index.php.

Federal Ministry of Economics and Technology (BMWi). 2013b. "EXIST-Rückblick."
Accessed June 18, 2013. http://www.exist.de/exist/rueckblick/index.php.

Feingold, M. 2005. *History of Universities.* Volume XX/2. Oxford: Oxford University
Press.

Fielden, S. L., and A. Dawe, A. 2004. "Entrepreneurship and Social Inclusion." *Women
in Management Review* 19 (3): 139–142.

Finkle, T. A., and D. Deeds. 2001. "Trends in the Market for Entrepreneurship Faculty,
1989–1998." *Journal of Business Venturing* 16 (6): 613–630.

Flint, T. P., and M. Rea. 2009. *The Oxford Handbook of Philosophical Theology.* New York: Oxford University Press.

Ford, D. 2001. "Trust and Knowledge Management: The Seeds of Success." Queen's KBE Centre for Knowledge-Based Enterprises Working Paper, No. 01-08.

Formaini, R. L. 2001. "The Engine of Capitalist Process: Entrepreneurs in Economic Theory." *Federal Reserve Bank of Dallas Economic and Financial Review,* 4th Quarter, 2–11.

Francks, R. 1979. "Omniscience, Omnipotence, and Pantheism." *Philosophy* 54 (209): 395–399.

Frank, M. W. 1998. "Schumpeter on Entrepreneurs and Innovation: A Reappraisal." *Journal of the History of Economic Thought* 20 (4): 505–516.

Franzen, G., and S. Moriarty. 2009. *The Science and Art of Branding.* New York: M.E. Sharpe.

Freke, T. 2002. *The Heart of Islam.* Hauppauge, NY: Barron's Educational Series.

Fuller, S. 1997. "The Secularization of Science and a New Deal for Science Policy." *Futures* 29 (6): 483–503.

Galloway, A. 2004. "Intimations of Everyday Life: Ubiquitous Computing and the City." *Cultural Studies* 18 (2–3): 384–408.

Gartner, W. B. 1990. "What Are We Talking About When We Talk About Entrepreneurship?" *Journal of Business Venturing* 5 (1): 15–28.

Genachowski, J. 2009. *Business Insider.* Accessed April 18, 2013. http://articles.businessinsider.com/2009-09-21/tech/30046158_1_chairman-julius-genachowski-internet-providers-national-broadband-plan.

Gennaioli, N., and A. Shleifer. 2007. "The Evolution of Common Law." *Journal of Political Economy* 115 (1): 43–68.

G-Forum. 2013. "G-Forum 17th Annual Interdisciplinary Entrepreneurship Conference." Accessed April 18, 2013. http://www.gforum2013.de/en/call-for-papers/.

Giersch, H. 1984. "The Age of Schumpeter." *The American Economic Review* 74 (2): 103–109.

Goldberg, J. C. P. 2005. "The Constitutional Status of Tort Law: Due Process and the Right to a Law for the Redress of Wrongs." *The Yale Law Journal* 115 (3): 524–627.

Google. 2013. "Glass." Accessed September 3, 2013. http://www.google.com/glass/start/.

Gorski, P. S. 2000. "Historicizing the Secularization Debate: Church, State, and Society in Late Medieval and Early Modern Europe, ca. 1300 to 1700." *American Sociological Review* 65 (1): 138–167.

Grant, E. 1996. *Planets, Stars, and Orbs: The Medieval Cosmos, 1200–1687*. Cambridge, UK: Cambridge University Press.

Grenz, S. J. 2000. *Theology for the Community of God*. Cambridge, UK: Wm. B. Eerdmans Publishing.

Grichnik, D., H. F. O. Von Kortzfleisch, and F. Magin. 2009. "Förderung von Entrepreneurship im Umfeld von Hochschulen: Notwendigkeit für eine ingenieurwissenschaftliche Vorgehensweise." In *Academic Entrepreneurship: Unternehmertum in der Forschung,* edited by A. Walter and M. Auer, 167–190. Wiesbaden: Gabler.

Grimm, V., F. Riedel, and E. Wolfstetter. 2003. "Low Price Equilibrium in Multi-Unit Auctions: The GSM Spectrum Auction in" Germany." *International Journal of Industrial Organization* 21 (2003): 1557–1569.

Online Etymology Dictionary. 2010. *s. v. "ubiquity."* Accessed February 26, 2013. http://dictionary.reference.com/browse/ubiquity.

Hartmann, J. 2011. *Westliche Regierungssysteme.* 3rd ed. Wiesbaden: Springer Verlag.

Hasso-Plattner-Institut. 2013. "Design Thinking." Accessed July 12, 2013.
http://www.hpi.uni-potsdam.de/d_school/designthinking.html.

Hausman, D. M. 1994. *The Philosophy of Economics*. 2nd ed. Cambridge, UK:
Cambridge University Press.

Hébert, R. F., and A. N. Link. 1989. "In Search of the Meaning of Entrepreneurship."
Small Business Economics 1:, 39–49.

Hébert, R. F., and A. N. Link. 2006. "The Entrepreneur as Innovator." *Journal of
Technology Transfer* 31: 589–597.

Hecker, B. 2012. *Europäisches Strafrecht*. 4th ed. Heidelberg: Springer.

Helmholz, R. H. 1990. "Continental Law and Common Law: Historical Strangers or
Companions?" *Duke Law Journal* 6: 1207–1228.

Henrekson, M. 2005. "Entrepreneurship: A Weak Link in the Welfare State?" *Industrial
and Corporate Change* 14 (3): 437–467.

Henrekson, M., and N. Rosenberg. 2000. *Incentives for Academic Entrepreneurship and
Economic Performance: Sweden and the United States*. Stockholm: Center for Business
and Policy Studies.

Hewlett-Packard. 2013. "HPEDU Deutschland – Kundenreferenzen. " Accessed August
18, 2013.
http://h41156.www4.hp.com/education/articles.aspx?cc=de&ll=de&id=772#SuccessSt
ories.

Hilbert, M., and P. López. 2011. "The World's Technological Capacity to Store,
Communicate, and Compute Information." *Science* 332 (6025): 60–65.

Hong, J. I., and J. A. Landay. 2004. "An Architecture for Privacy-Sensitive Ubiquitous
Computing." Proceedings of the Second International Conference on Mobile Systems,
Applications, and Services.

Hoselitz, B. F. 1960. "The Early History of Entrepreneurial Theory." In *Essays in Economic Thought: Aristotle to Marshall*, edited by J. J. Spengler and W. R. Allen, 234–258. Chicago: Rand McNally.

IBM. 2013. "Referenzberichte für Deutschland, Österreich und Schweiz." Accessed August 18, 2013. http://www-01.ibm.com/software/success/cssdb.nsf/topstoriesFM?OpenForm&Site=cssde&cty=de_de.

Iyigun, M. F., and A. L. Owen. 1998. "Risk, Entrepreneurship, and Human-Capital Accumulation." *The American Economic Review* 88 (2): 454–457.

Jones, O. 1983. "The Black Muslim Movement and the American Constitutional System." *Journal of Black Studies* 13 (4): 417–437.

Juris. 2012. "Introductory Act to the Civil Code." Accessed April 29, 2013. http://www.gesetze-im-internet.de/englisch_bgbeg/englisch_bgbeg.html#p0153.

Kantorowicz, E. 1997. *The King's Two Bodies: A Study in Mediaeval Political Theology.* Princeton, NY: Princeton University Press.

Keen, J. C. 1953. "Ramanuja, The Hindu Augustine." *Journal of Bible and Religion* 21 (1): 3–8.

King, A., and J. Brockington. 2005. *The Intimate Other: Love Divine in Indic Religious.* Hyderabad, India: Orient Longman.

Kirby, P. 2013. *Early Christian Writings.* Accessed Arpil 24, 2013. http://www.earlychristianwritings.com/1clement.html.

Kirzner, I. M. 1997. "Entrepreneurial Discovery and the Competitive Market Process: An Austrian Approach." *Journal of Economic Literature* 35 (1): 60–85.

Kirzner, I. M. 2005. "Information-Knowledge and Action-Knowledge." *Econ Journal Watch* 2 (1): 75–81.

Knight, F. H. 1942. "Profit and Entrepreneurial Functions." *The Journal of Economic History* 2: 126–132.

Kropholler, J. 2006. *Internationales Privatrecht.* 6th ed. Tübingen, Germany: Mohr Siebeck.

Langheinrich, M. 2003. "When Trust Does Not Compute – The Role of Trust in Ubiquitous Computing." Paper presented at the Fifth International Conference on Ubiquitous Computing, Seattle, Washington.

Lee, S. Y., R. Florida, and Z. Acs. 2004. "Creativity and Entrepreneurship: A Regional Analysis of New Firm Formation." *Regional Studies* 38 (8): 879–891.

Leibenstein, H. 1968. "Entrepreneurship and Development." *The American Economic Review* 58 (2): 72–83.

Lightfoot, J. B. 1868. *St. Paul's Epistle to the Philippians,* Vol. 1. London: Macmillan and Co.

Lightfoot, J. B. 1889. *The Apostolic Fathers.* 2nd ed. London: Macmillan and Co.

Littré, E. 1863. *Dictionnaire de la Langue Française.* Paris: L. Hachette et Cie.

Low, M. B., and I. C. MacMillan. 1988. "Entrepreneurship: Past Research and Future Challenges." *Journal of Management* 14 (2): 139–161.

Ludwig Maximilian University. 2013. "Über das Center." Accessed July 11, 2013. http://www.entrepreneurship-center.uni-muenchen.de/ueber_das_center/index.html.

Lünendonk. 2013. "Lünendonk®-Liste 2013: Führende IT-Beratungs-und Systemintegrations-Unternehmen in Deutschland." Accessed May 18, 2013. http://luenendonk-shop.de/out/pictures/0/lue_liste_u_pi_2013_it_beratung_f160513%282%29_fl.pdf.

Lyytinen, K. et al. 2004. "Surfing the Next Wave: Design and Implementation Challenges of Ubiquitous Computing Environments." *Communications of the Association for Information Systems* 14: 697–716.

Lyytinen, K., and Y. Yoo. 2002. "Issues and Challenges in Ubiquitous Computing." *Communications of the ACM* 45 (12): 63–65.

Magin, P., and H. F. Von Kortzfleisch. 2008. *Methoden und Instrumente des Scientific Entrepreneurship Engineering.* Lohmar-Cologne, Germany: Josef Eul.

Mattern, F. 2001. "The Vision and Technical Foundations of Ubiquitous Computing." *Upgrade* 2 (5): 3–6.

Mayer, R. C., J. H. Davis, and F. D. Schoorman. 1995. "An Integrative Model of Organizational Trust." *The Academy of Management Review* 20 (3): 709–734.

McCormick, M. 2000. "Why God Cannot Think: Kant, Omnipresence, and Consciousness." Accessed April 22, 2013. http://www.secularhumanism.org/library/philo/mccormick_3_1.htm.

Mommsen, T. E. 1951. "St. Augustine and the Christian Idea of Progress: The Background of the City of God." *Journal of the History of Ideas* 12 (3): 346–374.

Msg systems. 2007. "Success Story – Munich Re." Accessed August 18, 2013. http://www.msg-systems.com/fileadmin/user_upload/Branche_Insurance/Solutions/MunichRE_Gloria_DE.pdf.

Naqvi, E. 2012. *The Quran: With or Against the Bible?* Bloomington, IN: iUniverse.

Nerlove, M. 1999. "Transforming Economics: Theodore W. Schultz, 1902–1998: In Memoriam." *The Economic Journal* 109 (459): F726–F748.

Odgers, W. B. 1918. "Sir William Blackstone." *The Yale Law Journal* 27 (5): 599–618.

OECD. 2010. *Entrepreneurship and Migrants - Report by the OECD Working Party on SMEs and Entrepreneurship.* Paris: OECD.

Okanmibale, Y. I. 2012. "The Myth or Reality of Reincarnation from the Perspective of Islam." *Ilorin Journal of Religious Studies* 2 (2): 37–59.

Oliveira, L. 2000. "Commodification of Science and Paradoxes in Universities." *Science Studies* 13 (2): 23–36.

Penrose, E. T. 1995. *The Theory of the Growth of the Firm*. 2nd ed. New York: Oxford University Press.

Pew Research Center's Forum on Religion & Public Life. 2012a. *The Global Religious Landscape – Executive Summary*. Accessed April 30, 2013. http://www.pewforum.org/global-religious-landscape-exec.aspx.

Pew Research Center's Forum on Religion & Public Life. 2012b. *The Global Religious Landscape – Christians*. Accessed April 30, 2013. http://www.pewforum.org/global-religious-landscape-christians.aspx.

Prekop, P., and M. Burnett. 2003. "Activities, Context, and Ubiquitous Computing." *Computer Communications* 26 (11): 1168–1176.

Putterman, L. G., and R. S. Kroszner. 1996. *The Economic Nature of the Firm*. 2nd ed. Cambridge, UK: Cambridge University Press.

Reid, G. 1916. "Islam, an Appreciation." *The Biblical World* 48 (1): 7–17.

Richardson, A., and J. E. Bowden. 1983. *A New Dictionary of Christian Theology*. London: SCM Press.

Roberts, A., and J. Donaldson, J. 1870. *The Writings: Translations of the Writings of the Fathers Down to A. D. 325*. Edinburgh: T. & T. Clark.

Robins, K., and F. Webster. 2002. *The Virtual University?* Oxford: Oxford University Press.

Rockley, A., and C. Cooper. 2012. *Managing Enterprise Content*. 2nd ed. Berkeley, CA: New Riders.

Rothaermel, F. T., S. D. Agung, and L. Jiang. 2007. "University Entrepreneurship: A Taxonomy of the Literature." *Industrial and Corporate Change* 16 (4): 691–791.

Rüegg, W. 2011. *A History of the University in Europe.* Vol. 4, *Universities Since 1945.* Cambridge, UK: Cambridge University Press.

Saha, D., and A. Mukherjee. 2003. "Pervasive Computing: A Paradigm for the 21st Century." *Computer* 36 (3): 25–31.

Saha, D., A. Mukherjee, and S. Bandyopadhyay. 2003. *Networking Infrastructure for Pervasive Computing: Enabling Technologies and Systems.* Dordrecht, The Netherlands: Springer.

Samuelson, P. A. 1983. "Thünen at Two Hundred." *Journal of Economic Literature* 21 (4): 1468–1488.

Sandelin, J. 2004. "The Story of the Stanford Industrial / Research Park." Paper prepared for the International Forum of University Science Park, China.

Schaff, P., 2007. *Nicene and Post-Nicene Fathers: First Series.* New York: Cosimo, Inc.

Scheruhn, P. D. H.-J. 2013. "Atos-Siemens-Zertifikat." Accessed July 10, 2013. http://hscheruhn.hs-harz.de/lehre/lehre_siemens.html.

Schultz, T. W. 1975. "The Value of the Ability to Deal with Disequilibria." *Journal of Economic Literature* 13 (3): 827–846.

Schultz, T. W. 1980. "Investment in Entrepreneurial Ability." *The Scandinavian Journal of Economics* 82 (4): 437–448.

Sivananda, S. S. 1998. *God Exists.* World Wide Web ed. Uttar Pradesh, India: The Divine Life Trust Society.

Smalley, B. 1961. Review of *The King's Two Bodies. A Study in Mediaeval Political Theology,* by Ernst H. Kantorowicz. *The Past and Present* 20: 30–35.

Spengler, J. J. 1954. "Richard Cantillon: First of the Moderns." *Journal of Political Economy* 62 (4): 281–295.

Stanford Encyclopedia of Philosophy. 2010. s. v. *"sovereignty."* Accessed April 29, 2013. http://plato.stanford.edu/entries/sovereignty/.

Sternberg, R., U. Brixy, and A. Vorderwuelbecke. 2012. *Global Entrepreneurship Monitor.* Hannover, Germany: Institute of Economic and Cultural Geography.

Stevenson, H. H., and J. C. Jarillo. 1990. A Paradigm of Entrepreneurship: Entrepreneurial Management. *Strategic Management Journal* 11: 17–27.

Stockl, A. 1858. *Die speculative Lehre vom Menschen und ihre Geschichte.* Würzburg, Germany: Verlag der Stahel'schen Buch- und Kunsthandlung.

Strassner, M., and T. Schoch. 2002. "Today's Impact of Ubiquitous Computing on Business Processes." Paper presented at International Conference on Pervasive Computing, Zürich, Switzerland.

Strauss, S. 2002. "The Master's Narrative: Swami Sivananda and the Transnational Production of Yoga." *Journal of Folklore Research* 39 (2/3): 217–241.

Strong, A. H. 1907. *Systematic Theology.* Philadelphia: American Baptist Publication Society.

Strong, A. H. 1908. *Outlines of Systematic Theology.* Philadelphia: The Griffith & Rowland Press.

Sylter Runde. 2007. *"Scientific Entrepreneurship – Was sollen Wissenschaftler noch alles richten?* Westerland / Sylt, Germany.

Sylter Runde. 2013. *Mission.* Accessed July 17, 2013. http://www.sylter-runde.de/mission.html.

Thillainathan, N. 2010. "Four Paths to Freedom: Hindu Concepts in Counselling." *Psychotherapy in Australia* 16 (3): 73–74.

Topping, R. 2002. "Transformation and the Will in St. Anselm's Proslogion: A Response to Augustine's Articulation of the Problem of Human Evil." *The European Legacy* 7 (1): 33–43.

Tschannen, O. 1991. "The Secularization Paradigm: A Systematization." *Journal for the Scientific Study of Religion* 30 (4): 395–415.

T-Systems, 2013. "Referenzen." Accessed August 18, 2013. http://www.t-systems.de/referenzen/referenzen/753568.

Twaalfhoven, W. M. 2004. *Red Paper on Entrepreneurship*. Hilversum, The Netherlands: European Forum for Entrepreneurship Research.

University of Chicago. 2013. "Ronald H. Coase." Accessed June 7, 2013. http://www.law.uchicago.edu/faculty/coase.

Unnik, W. C. V. 1951. "1 Clement 34 and the 'Sanctus.'" *Vigiliae Christianae* 5 (4): 204–248.

Van der Sijde, P. C., A. Ridder, J. Van Benthem, and A. Groen. 2002. "Entrepreneurship and Entrepreneurship Stimulation at the University of Twente." In *Infrastructures for Academic Spin-off Companies,* edited by Sijde et al. n.p.: Limencop, CEE.

Venkatesan, S. 2006. "Shifting Balances in a 'Craft Community': The Mat Weavers of Pattamadai, South India." *Contributions to Indian Sociology* 40 (1): 63–89.

Vesper, K. H., and W. B. Gartner. 1997. "Measuring Progress in Entrepreneurship Education." *Journal of Business Venturing* 12 (5): 403–421.

Viale, R., and H. Etzkowitz. 2005. "Third Academic Revolution: Polyvalent Knowledge; The DNA of the Triple Helix." Paper presented at the Fifth Triple Helix Conference, Turin, Italy.

Von Hippel, E. 1988. *The Sources of Innovation*. New York: Oxford University Press.

Von Kortzfleisch, H. F. O. 2011. *Scientific Entrepreneurship: Reflections on Success of 10 Years EXIST*. Lohmar-Cologne, Germany: Josef Eul.

Von Mises, L. 1946. *Bureaucracy*. 3rd ed. New Haven: Yale University Press.

Wadhwa, V., R. Aggarwal, K. Holly, and A. Salkever. 2009. *The Anatomy of an Entrepreneur – Family Background and Motivation.* n.p.: Ewing Marion Kauffman Foundation.

Walker, D. A., 1986. Walras's Theory of the Entrepreneur. *De Economist,* 134(1), pp. 1-24.

Walras, L., 2005. *Studies in Applied Economicss.* New York: Taylor & Francis.

Weiser, M., 1991. The Computer for the 21st Century. *Scientific American*, September, pp. 94-104.

Weiser, M. 1993. "Some Computer Science Issues in Ubiquitous Computing." *Communications of the ACM* 36 (7): 75–84.

Weiser, M., R. Gold, and J. S. Brown. 1999. "The Origins of Ubiquitous Computing Research at PARC in the late 1980s." *IBM Systems Journal* 38 (4): 693–696.

Wennekers, S., and R. Thurik. 1999. "Linking Entrepreneurship and Economic Growth." *Small Business Economics* 13 (1): 27–55.

Wierenga, E. R. 1989. *The Nature of God: An Inquiry Into Divine Attributes.* Ithaca, NY: Cornell University Press.

World Economic Forum. 2009. *Educating the Next Wave of Entrepreneurs. Unlocking Entrepreneurial Capabilities to Meet the Global Challenges of the 21st Century.* Davos-Klosters, Switzerland: World Economic Forum.

Yeung, H. W.-C. 2009. "Transnationalizing Entrepreneurship: A Critical Agenda for Economic Geography." *Progress in Human Geography* 33 (2): 210–235.

Yoeli, M. E. I. R. 1968. "Mot, the Canaanite God, as Symbol of the Leper." *Bulletin of the New York Academy of Medicine* 44 (8): 1057–1067.